Samuel French Acting Edition

The Luck of the Irish

by Kirsten Greenidge

SAMUELFRENCH.COM   SAMUELFRENCH.CO.UK

FOR PRODUCTION ENQUIRIES

UNITED STATES AND CANADA
Info@SamuelFrench.com
1-866-598-8449

UNITED KINGDOM AND EUROPE
Plays@SamuelFrench.co.uk
020-7255-4302

Each title is subject to availability from Samuel French, depending upon country of performance. Please be aware that *THE LUCK OF THE IRISH* may not be licensed by Samuel French in your territory. Professional and amateur producers should contact the nearest Samuel French office or licensing partner to verify availability.

MUSIC USE NOTE

Licensees are solely responsible for obtaining formal written permission from copyright owners to use copyrighted music in the performance of this play and are strongly cautioned to do so. If no such permission is obtained by the licensee, then the licensee must use only original music that the licensee owns and controls. Licensees are solely responsible and liable for all music clearances and shall indemnify the copyright owners of the play(s) and their licensing agent, Samuel French, against any costs, expenses, losses and liabilities arising from the use of music by licensees. Please contact the appropriate music licensing authority in your territory for the rights to any incidental music.

IMPORTANT BILLING AND CREDIT REQUIREMENTS

If you have obtained performance rights to this title, please refer to your licensing agreement for important billing and credit requirements.

THE LUCK OF THE IRISH was first commissioned by South Coast Repertory Theatre, Costa Mesa, CA, and commissioned again by the Huntington Theatre Company, Boston, MA. The play opened at The Huntington Theater Company April 11, 2012 and was directed by Melia Bensussen.

THE *LUCK OF THE IRISH* was produced by LTC3 at Lincoln Center's Clare Tow Theater in New York, New York, February 11, 2013. It was directed by Rebecca Taichman.

CHARACTERS

(in order of appearance)

NESSA CHARLES – very early thirties, black, Hannah's younger sister; the Taylors' granddaughter.

HANNAH DAVIS – mid thirties, black, the Taylor's granddaughter

MR. DONOVAN – early eighties, first generation Irish American

JOE DONOVAN – very early thirties, Mr. Donovan's younger self

PATTY ANN DONOVAN, very early thirties, second generation Irish American, Joe's wife

LUCY TAYLOR – mid thirties, Boston Brahmin black

REX TAYLOR – mid thirties, but older than Lucy, Lucy's husband, tranplant from Northern Virginia, black

RICH DAVIS – same age as Hannah, Hannah's husband, transplant from DC

MRS. DONOVAN – early eighties, an elderly Patty Ann

MILES – nine, Hannah and Rich's son

OFF STAGE VOICES – Two young girls

SETTING

A medium sized suburban town on the outskirts of Boston, Massachusetts, which was formerly colonial and brimming with old New England stock, but by the very early twentieth century, predominantly Irish Catholic. By the time we meet this town, the Italians have arrived, followed by bands of others throughout the twentieth century. By the early twenty first century it is not so much diverse as it is tolerant of those who are "other" as it is still predominantly white.

The action takes place in the late 1950s and 2000s.

DIALECTS/ACCENTS

Hannah and Nessa speak with a standard American accent for the most part. Being black in America, however, they wear "the veil" well, and their speech is fluid and not inaccessibly "bougie".

Lucy should speak with a Boston Brahmin accent. Akin to Rose Kennedy. Joe, Patty Ann, Mr. Donovan, and Mrs. Donovan should speak with Boston accents.

Rex should have a Virginia sway to his speech.

Rich should have a standard American accent.

Miles should have a standard accent, but he prefers to make some of his words "cool".

AUTHOR'S NOTES

When constructing this play, I was aware that I wanted to tell the story of a rather complicated scenario that has proven difficult to research while keeping the essentials of the play as human and vibrant as they exist in my head. Therefore, the phenomenon of "ghost buying" is not the subject of this play. There are many facts and legal loopholes that render "ghost buying" fascinating, but which began to clog my vision for the play. So I began to configure a play that examines, in short scenes that accumulate and accrue into a story, how one group of people experience the phenomena and how its effect ripples through to subsequent generations. That being said, I deliberately created a play that acts more like a glass prism: all slants and angles surrounding a seemingly simple core. As such we see different configurations of characters grappling with the dreams and hopes and choices that were made with all the greatest intentions half a century earlier.

Before I built a wall I'd ask to know
What I was walling in or walling out,
And to whom I was like to give offense.
        – "Mending Wall", Robert Frost

For Grandma and Grandpa Dance. And for my daughter, Katia.
Please remember that wherever you are is where you belong.
Don't let anyone convince you otherwise.

ACT I

(Note: While I am a firm and ardent believer in "the play should speak for itself", please read the Author's Notes that precede Act I...)

(In darkness, the sound of wind, soft.)

*(Lights rise on **NESSA** and **HANNAH**, who fold flowered paper napkins at a picnic table; plastic liter bottles of soda sit out in the midday sun.)*

NESSA. She wouldn't like paper.

HANNAH. I'm supposed to use cloth outside?

NESSA. Just saying.

HANNAH. *(holding up a napkin)* They have flowers. And I can't use cloth outside. *(calling out gruffly)* Hey. Get off of there. *(to **NESSA**)* He's on a patch, but I don't think it's working.

NESSA. He didn't bite me this time.

HANNAH. He was saying hello. He gets excited.

NESSA. I meant I think he's doing good, a patch is good.

HANNAH. It's that new school that hypes him up. This whole year, by the end of the day, he's all hyped –. I told Rich, I told him these schools don't know, they just don't –. But Rich doesn't get it. Rich loved school –

NESSA. DC.

HANNAH. Chocolate City.

NESSA. I bet he went to the prom.

HANNAH. Purple tux, purple shoes, purple top hat.

NESSA. Now that's black, right there. All one color like that.

HANNAH. Right? So he wasn't an only so he doesn't – *(Calling)* I said get off of that and I mean it right now. *(To* NESSA*)* I sound like I'm from the East side, screaming at my kid like that, but he always finds the craziest place to be. Grandma's skin would crawl, if she could hear.

*(*NESSA *look at* HANNAH.*)*

NESSA. Oh Grandma can hear all right. She's still around.

HANNAH. If the kids hear you talking about that ghosty spooky stuff they won't sleep for a week.

NESSA. It's not spooky, it's beautiful. And you can't tell me you haven't felt something, felt either of them living here in their house.

*(*NESSA *looks at* HANNAH.*)*

HANNAH. Last time their Auntie Nessa came and filled their heads I had to go from room to room every night because of nightmares.

NESSA. Grandma, Grandpa, they're both still here. It's a sign.

HANNAH. *Not* the button thing again, Ness.

NESSA. You keep finding them all over the house, that's what you said.

HANNAH. She lived here for fifty years, of course we're going to find her stuff everywhere.

NESSA. She kept them in that jar, not all over the place.

HANNAH. Grandma Lucy was the only person I've met who collected buttons.

NESSA. Peculiar, that's what she called it.

HANNAH. *(calling)* Miles.

MILES. What did I just *SAY*?? *(to* NESSA*)* Thank God Lucy J doesn't act like. I couldn't manage two of those, I couldn't.

NESSA. Who's coming to this shindig, anyway?

(Beat.)

HANNAH. I still can't believe it not even a month, both she and Grandpa Gone–. I just thought a little something would be nice, since it's her birthday.

NESSA. She never would have planned a birthday party for herself where people could tramp all over her backyard. There's already a dry patch –

HANNAH. Get out of here talking about a dry patch. The lawn is not high on my list, Ness, of stuff about this house I have to deal with.

NESSA. It's half my house, too. Give me half that list.

HANNAH. Don't worry about it. This is why I am a very good big sister. Rich and I moved in so you don't have to worry about any of it.

(NESSA *looks at* HANNAH.)

NESSA. I don't understand why we have to invite people to this birthday. Most of her friends are dead.

HANNAH. No, they're not. There's Grace from across the street.

NESSA. Grace was always a good cook. I hope you're on your game for this. Did you make the potato salad with the mayonnaise or the vinegar? Cause everyone around here eats it with the mayonnaise. White people *love* mayonnaise.

HANNAH. Grandma, herself, ate mayonnaise.

NESSA. Fifty years you'd think this neighborhood would have changed just a little.

HANNAH. Nope. We're still the only flies in the buttermilk up around here.

(NESSA *smiles.*)

(*They work.*)

NESSA. So us and Grace.

HANNAH. ...And...I invited the Coopers from down near the park.

NESSA. The Coopers built a pool, did you see that?

HANNAH. You'd think she'd built a Roman bath the way Mrs. Cooper goes on and on. It's a hole in the ground with tile, that's what it is.

NESSA. Looked great to me. That's what this yard needs, a pool. I'll pay half.

HANNAH. Pay half. That's generous. You don't even live here.

NESSA. I could. I'm sick of my roommate anyway. I could move in.

HANNAH. You ask for that raise, then you could pay for the whole thing yourself.

NESSA. I'm waiting for the right time.

HANNAH. Riiight. New shoes?

NESSA. ...why?

HANNAH. Are those. New shoes.

NESSA. If you like them, then yes. If you're gonna make some comment about them then I'd rather not say.

HANNAH. Just think of all the new shoes you could buy if you got that raise.

NESSA. Next time. When the timing's –

HANNAH. Red ones, green ones –

NESSA. The timing wasn't right to ask, you know that, I've told you.

HANNAH. Orange ones, *boots, galoshes...*

NESSA. I'm serious.

(**HANNAH** *looks at* **NESSA**.)

(**NESSA** *looks at* **HANNAH**.)

You'd know more about it if we actually...talked...like at lunch, or something. We could have lunch.

(**NESSA** *looks down at her work*.)

(**HANNAH** *looks down at her work*.)

(**HANNAH** *looks up at* **NESSA**, *then back down at her work*.)

HANNAH. If Mrs. Cooper traps me in the cereal aisle one more time to go on about that pool . She always gets me right near the Fruit Loops – Last week she was going on and on about chlorine and I'm nodding and smiling and I look down and I realize the kids are gone and I try nicely to *stop* talking about chlorine before the PA system calls my name and lets the whole world I lost my kids when I see them at the end of the aisle. And their shirts are all wet and they're carrying baskets and Mrs. Cooper's in her own world of filters and pool boys and the kids are getting closer and I see they're drenched and I get a look inside those baskets they're lugging and I see those two went and freed live lobsters from the deli.

(NESSA *smiles, laughs, wags her head.*)

HANNAH. Mrs. Cooper's got one hell of a stink eye.

NESSA. That's sweet. They're sweet. You raised some sweet kids.

HANNAH. She's got the old lady judgment mouth, too. That's the last thing I need is her gabbing about how badly my kids, how wild they are every time I take them out –

NESSA. It's not every time.

HANNAH. You knock on Mrs. Cooper's door and tell her that please.

NESSA. You should be proud, you've taught them to be socially conscious.

HANNAH. I wish I'd taught them to look for sales, those lobsters were 8.99 a pound. Mrs. Cooper is one chatty cathy, but that's what these neighbors do, they try to chat you up and talk your ears off.

NESSA. Um, I think talking to your neighbors in the supermarket is called being polite.

HANNAH. It's nosy. If Mrs. Cooper breathes one more word about that pool the next time there's a neighborhood thing I'm gonna tell Miles to pee in there, I swear to God.

NESSA. That's lovely. So three people. We're having a second memorial in picnic form for three people

(**HANNAH** *looks at* **NESSA**.)

HANNAH. *And… I…*invited the Donovans, too. Since they couldn't come to the memorial. Grandma would have liked that.

(**NESSA** *moans.*)

HANNAH. I invited the Donovans, so be nice.

NESSA. *(A whine)* Han-nah.

HANNAH. Don't whine, Nessa, you sound worse than the kids.

NESSA. You should have asked me.

HANNAH. I. Thought I did.

NESSA. Well you didn't.

HANNAH. What's the big deal?

NESSA. They have that mothy smell.

HANNAH. Nessa.

NESSA. They weren't *our* friends we shouldn't have to invite them.

HANNAH. They were the first people grandma and grandpa met here. And she loved it here. She raised mom and Auntie June here, she raised you and me here after mom left us to do all her hug the trees shove it to the man stuff and Daddy was God knows where.

NESSA. It's just… They have that mothy smell. That digs under your skin, your bone, and makes you want to –

(*Wind.* **MR. DONOVAN** *has appeared out of nowhere.*)

(*The wind subsides.*)

MR. DONOVAN. H…hello?

(*Both women jump, turn, and see* **MR. DONOVAN**.)

(*When he sees them, he takes his hat off, grips it in his hands.*)

(*Note: The name "Balich" is pronounced "Bay-lick"*)

HANNAH. Mr. Donovan?

NESSA. Hello, Mr. Donovan.

MR. DONOVAN. I'm…I'm sorry, I'm a little early –

HANNAH. Nonsense, please, here, have a seat.

(She moves picnic preparations so MR. DONOVAN *can sit, but he stands, hat in hand.)*

MR. DONOVAN. Oh, I don't know –

HANNAH. Don't be shy, Mr. Donovan. Where's Mrs. Donovan? On her way around the house?

MR. DONOVAN. Mrs. Donovan –

HANNAH. Don't tell me she's sick again.

MR. DONOVAN. No, no, she –

HANNAH. She just got over that cold she said, when I talked to her on the phone. There's nothing worse than a summer cold. Please. Sit. Nessa can get you a drink.

MR. DONOVAN. Oh NO.

NESSA. I can get you a drink, no trouble –

MR. DONOVAN. I. Shouldn't –. Mrs. Donovan is –.

*(*HANNAH *looks at* MR. DONOVAN.*)*

*(*MR. DONOVAN *looks at* HANNAH.*)*

HANNAH. …Are you alright, Mr. Donovan?

MR. DONOVAN. *(to himself, gripping his hat)* Maybe I should, maybe I should sit down.

HANNAH. Have something to drink.

MR. DONOVAN. I, I –

NESSA. We've got coke.

MR. DONOVAN. Coke…

NESSA. But we've also got the hard stuff.

*(*HANNAH *jabs* NESSA.*)*

HANNAH. Would you like a coke, Mr. Donovan?

(The sound of a car horn. MR. DONOVAN *seems confused, looks toward his car, doesn't move.)*

(HANNAH nudges NESSA again to get another drink NESSA does.)

(Wind, a soft billow.)

(NESSA hands MR. DONOVAN a drink.)

(MR. DONOVAN puts it to his lips and drinks, without stopping for air.)

(HANNAH and NESSA watch.)

(When he is done, he places the soda can on the table.)

(Beat.)

(HANNAH nudges NESSA, who gets another drink.)

(MR. DONOVAN looks down at the soda can.)

MR. DONOVAN. Tonic.

(A soft billow.)

MR. DONOVAN. I remember when this was five cents. You could go down the Balich Five and Ten and you could get a whole bottle. Glass bottle. Ice cold and the sides would rub off on your fingers, make them wet. They were good people, the Balich's. Good, good, but. But...

(He looks at NESSA and HANNAH.)

(He loses himself in thought.)

(NESSA and HANNAH stand, not knowing quite what to do.)

MR. DONOVAN. Your grandmother. Rest her soul. She'd remember. Five cents.

(MR. DONOVAN puts on his hat.)

MR. DONOVAN. I don't go in for that racial stuff. I want you to know.

HANNAH. Is there someone we can call for you, Mr. Donovan? To maybe pick you up?

MR. DONOVAN. No. *NO.* Mrs. Donovan's in the car –

HANNAH. In the car? Well that's ridiculous, tell her to come around –

MR. DONOVAN. She. She's staying in the car.

(**MR. DONOVAN** *looks to* **HANNAH,** *then* **NESSA.**)

MR. DONOVAN. Such nice girls. Just like your grandmother…

HANNAH. Can I get you something else, Mr. Donovan?

NESSA. You can take it to go.

MR. DONOVAN. It's the house. She says it's still ours.

HANNAH. Who?

MR. DONOVAN. Mrs. Donovan says the communions, they're coming up, and with Doctor Taylor and your grandmother gone Mrs. Donovan got to thinking this house would be a good place to, to celebrate the communions. Our last grandaughter's, got us wrapped around her pinky finger and Mrs. Donovan –. I always said don't go bothering them. But when we saw in the paper they'd passed away Mrs. Donovan got to thinking how nice a party would be in this yard. And she thinks the whole place shouldn't go to just anyone –

HANNAH. What's that mean?

MR. DONOVAN. It's all coming out wrong. She makes me nervous. She sent me to tell you she wants it as her own.

HANNAH. This house was not left to "just anyone" Mr. Donovan –

NESSA. It was left to *us.*

MR. DONOVAN. Yes, see, well, that's the thing. This house, when Dr. and Mrs. Taylor –

(**LUCY** *enters.*)

(*She begins to prepare for cocktails.*)

HANNAH. Our grandparents –

MR. DONOVAN. Bought this house, there was an arrangement. That In order to buy it, they. There was a deal.

(**REX** *enters with* **JOE** *and* **PATTY ANN.**)

HANNAH. A deal?

(REX, LUCY, JOE, *and* PATTY ANN *laugh, jovially.*)

MR. DONOVAN. We, we. Yes. We, bought this house for them –

HANNAH. No, Mr. Donovan –

MR. DONOVAN. And now, now Mrs. Donovan, she says she wants it back, now that your grandparents are gone. I'm so sorry.

(Cocktail laughter.)

(A car horn.)

MR. DONOVAN. She's...waiting, I...need to...

(MR. DONOVAN *exits.*)

(NESSA *looks at* HANNAH.)

NESSA. Those buttons, Han, I told you. They're a sign.

(HANNAH *looks at* NESSA.)

(NESSA *looks at* HANNAH.)

(Wind.)

(Cocktail laughter.)

(HANNAH *exits into the house.*)

(NESSA *follows.*)

PATTY ANN. Well I did, that's exactly what I said to him, I said, "Mr. Balich," I said –

JOE. She's got the gift of the gab, my wife, can't you tell?

LUCY. Oh now.

PATTY ANN. He loves my stories, don't you let him fool you.

REX. *(To* JOE*)* You might put your foot in it, now.

JOE. Of course I love your stories. I'm the luckiest man in the world when it comes to her stories because they're the quickest way to a nap.

(All laugh except PATTY ANN*.)*

PATTY ANN. Well ten cents just seems out of this world, when I can go to the A and P and buy up all the coca-colas I want for just five cents each. Mr. Balich's making a horrible mistake.

REX. Of all the wonders I'm sure are inside Balich's five and ten, the most notable merchandise my wife comes home with after her visits are buttons.

LUCY. I think we need touch ups, Rex. *(to* PATTY ANN *and* JOE*)* I'd driven out to see where the girls might go to school. I only stopped on my way back here, in to Boston.

PATTY ANN. He is, Mr. Balich is making a terrible mistake. Now Lucy's been there. Lucy agrees with me, don't you Lucy?

REX. One school trip leads to almost a jam jar full of buttons?

LUCY. There is more than one school in that town, Rex. *(to* PATTY ANN *and* JOE*)* Before we decided on the Vitello's house, we weren't sure which neighborhood might suit us best.

PATTY ANN. Ah.

REX. But in the end it was the beauty of the house that won us. A nice family house.

LUCY. We're so glad you could come to discuss it.

PATTY ANN. Of course.

REX. All this way into the city it can be quite a hike –

JOE. Hop skip and a jump is all it is. I can't believe I've never been over this side of Boston sooner, now that I see it. Beautiful. All the brick, all the stone –

PATTY ANN. It's lovely.

LUCY. On the small side.

REX. We never thought we'd be here long. I always thought I'd start my practice down in Virginia where I'm from, but Lucy –

LUCY. Well I was born and raised here in Boston, why would I want to move to the Boondocks?

(Pause.)

PATTY ANN. It's a lovely apartment.

JOE. Indeed it is.

LUCY. Do you know the Vitellos?

JOE. Patty Ann here went to school with the wife.

REX. Their house in Bellington, it's a real winner. There's the Vitellos on that street and I think a Greek couple a few streets over so –

LUCY. So, a Negro family wouldn't be such a shock –

PATTY ANN. Well the schools up the hill are excellent.

LUCY. Oh, all the schools are. I drove out to see each one. I didn't make a spectacle, but each school I surely did visit and. I guess I made a habit of stopping, on my way back here, to do a little shopping.

REX. She's already filled half a jam jar with buttons from those trips.

JOE. If ever the world gets too much for you, my dear mother used to say, peep through a button hole: calm you down in no time at all, that perspective.

PATTY ANN. Mr. Balich's lucky his doors are still open, let me tell you.

LUCY. The wives have Mr. Balich on a short leash, it seems.

PATTY ANN. For years he's had the best prices in town, but now.Well you've been in, I'd think you'd agree with me.

(Slight, very slight, beat.)

LUCY. Well I was in right after Mr. Balich tried to raise stockings up a nickel and you would have thought that President Eisenhower had declared World War Three.

PATTY ANN. Well see, there, because stockings up a nickel makes no business sense.

JOE. Mr. Balich'll be in the bread line if he starts listening to my wife about business sense.

PATTY ANN. I wouldn't get so high and mighty, you.

LUCY. How about another drink?

*(**REX** rises to the small portable glass bar.)*

LUCY. Would either of you like another –

REX. Here, here we go –

PATTY ANN. I know from business sense, Mr. Joseph Patrick Donovan and don't you forget it.

REX. *(Raising the bottle)* Who would like another?

(JOE *keeps his eyes focused and leveled on* PATTY ANN.)

JOE. Just a touch more.

LUCY. Good, me too.

(REX *makes drinks.*)

(PATTY ANN *keeps her eyes focused and leveled on* JOE.)

PATTY ANN. Yes. A touch more would be lovely. Thank you.

REX. We're just so glad you could come and talk this over.

JOE. Well why not?

LUCY. We've been down this road before. Over in –

REX. We don't need to –

LUCY. Over in Newton.

JOE. *Newton* –

PATTY ANN. That was you?

REX. Luckily –

LUCY. That was us. Yes –

PATTY ANN. Joe, you never told me that was them.

JOE. I knew you'd had a house fire, that you had to leave because of a house fire –

LUCY. 'Waited until the moving van peeled off and nearly burned the house down –

PATTY ANN. The paper said it was a Negro family but, well, I guess you never really put a face –

REX. Luckily, no one was hurt –

LUCY. And we're just happy we're meeting with you now –

PATTY ANN. *(Part impressed, part something else)* Newton wee.

REX. Yes, Lucy's right, we're very happy we're all meeting together now –

LUCY. If this works out –

REX. We're really hoping this will work out –

JOE. How can it not work –?

PATTY ANN. Lawns as wide as the sea over there in Newton.

LUCY. We. Just.

REX. It's the children we're –

PATTY ANN. Two boys, isn't it?

LUCY. Girls.

JOE. Ah. You'd better be careful with them, Rex.

LUCY. Two girls. Tasha's the elder. The baby –

REX. She's not a baby, she's got orders in to the tooth fairy as we speak.

LUCY. The younger is named June.

PATTY ANN. *(not sincere, but not quite insincere, either)* How sweet.

JOE. When they hit thirteen only way to manage them is to lock the doors and windows. Throw away the key.

LUCY. And you? You've got–?

PATTY ANN. Three girls, three boys.

LUCY. Oh. My.

JOE. We're blessed.

REX. To the next generation then.

>   *(All raise their glasses.)*

>   *(Beat.)*

>   *(They drink.)*

>   *(LUCY stops first.)*

LUCY. I don't know how I'd manage with six.

PATTY ANN. You manage.

JOE. Girls.

LUCY. I don't know how I manage with two.

REX. They're really very good girls –

JOE. With girls? You lock the door is how you manage –

PATTY ANN. Yes, you just said.

JOE. You keep the daughters in, let the sons out. That's how the peace is kept. Patty Ann here could have six*teen* more and the peace would be kept, let me tell you locks on every window and every door. Who was it said fences make good neighbors?

PATTY ANN. It wasn't anybody, Joe. It was the newspaper.

LUCY. No. It was Frost.

(JOE *and* PATTY ANN *look at her.*)

LUCY. Isn't it? Robert –?

(REX *gives* LUCY *a look.*)

LUCY. Well maybe it wasn't.

(REX *gives* LUCY *another look.*)

(LUCY*'s eyes meet* REX*'s, then refocus in front of her.*)

(LUCY *takes a gulp of her drink.*)

JOE. Fences make good *families*. That's what I aim to mean.

REX. Well that's what we want. To raise our family–

PATTY ANN. Of course.

JOE. Patty and me, we don't go in for the racial stuff.

PATTY ANN. I just said that, Joe.

JOE. We believe in equality.

PATTY ANN. That's right.

JOE. Winds of change. Because Patty and me, we believe what a man earns is his, rightly his –

PATTY ANN. And what a man loses he thinks is forever his.

LUCY. Like I said, we've been down this road before –

JOE. And what a man chooses to do with what he earns, well, well…

PATTY ANN. They understand, Joe.

REX. So. We put up the cash –

JOE. Cash?

REX. Well, yes. For the Vitello place. And the title will be in your name initially. One copy to the Town Hall, and it passes by the right eyes, through the right hands, and the other copy to you. Then you transfer that title over and the house would be ours. The Vitello's to you to us. Half a week tops, and it's all done, all taken care of.

JOE. Cash.

PATTY ANN. Yes, Joe, they just said. *(to* LUCY *and* REX*):* Sometimes I think there's potatoes in this one's ears.

REX. Cash for you to buy the Vitello house, and then also to compensate you, for your help.

JOE. ...Because I say, I say a man wants to buy his own house, his own castle, like Rex here is trying to do, then, then, then I say this is the very place for that to happen. I say, what was the war all about –

PATTY ANN. Joe.

JOE. No, no, I'm, I'm making a point here what was the war –

PATTY ANN. We're happy to think it over, is what my –

JOE. A man works and earns a man oughta be able to buy a house, that's what I, that's all I –. Patty and me, we don't go in for any of that racial nonsense.

PATTY ANN. You're repeating yourself, dear.

JOE. It's because I mean it. From the moment I heard your predicament – I thought to myself well, that's a shame.

LUCY. The light bulbs were still cool. We'd just turned them on, it was dusk –

REX. So you can imagine, we're more than a little worried –

JOE. Patty and me understand completely. When John down at Atlantic Construction –

PATTY ANN. Now Joe, I'm sure the Taylors don't want to see our woes cut up and served on a plate –

JOE. When we ran into our trouble and I went to see about a little help, a little advance on my pay, and he – oh, he's a clever one, John, I'm not surprised you two are, uh, acquainted, Rex –

REX. John does alright.

JOE. More than alright. A deal here, a deal there. John's kids've all got straight teeth. Like little white wash boards straight as arrows. I've noticed. I've checked.

REX. To John, then, for bringing us all together –

(All raise their glasses and drink. Beat.)

JOE. When we ran into our trouble –

PATTY ANN. *Joe.*

JOE. and I ended up in John's office, hat in hand, hand shaking like a leaf – you ever feel that way? You ever –? There's supposed to be gold paving on the streets but under your own personal roof it's wailing and crooked teeth and–. And John's clever, John took one look at me and said "Ya know, Joe, there's this fella, this colored fella who can help you out. Sure as silk he can – "

PATTY ANN. They know the story, Joe, no need to –

JOE. "There's this colored fella with green flowing out his pockets like you wouldn't believe," John says –

PATTY ANN. We're happy to consider it, is what he means –

LUCY. Oh, I hope so, Rex and I both hope you'll say yes –

JOE. Fast friends. That's what I say.

LUCY. – I mean Rex and I first looked at that house in the dark.

JOE. That's a strange time to show a house.

REX. It was dark because it was after work.

LUCY. *(to* REX*)* It was the dead of night. *(to* PATTY ANN *and* JOE*)* We don't want to trick, you understand –

PATTY ANN. Of course not.

REX. How about a touch up?

LUCY. I want to be frank.

JOE. Of course you do.

LUCY. The neighbors. We. We just want to move in and then maybe once they meet us, meet the girls, because they really are good –

*(*REX *cuts* LUCY *off by pouring her some more to drink.)*

REX. Lucy doesn't want to see our girls go through that again.

PATTY ANN. Of course not.

REX. We're thinking once we move in, we can show everyone –

LUCY. We just couldn't get anywhere going the more uh conventional –

PATTY ANN. Sure –

JOE. A man dreams big and he pays.

PATTY ANN. Shh.

REX. Your name on the title.

PATTY ANN. And the money –

LUCY. Oh, we take care of the money.

PATTY ANN. *Our* money. When do we get *our* money?

JOE. A man dreams big –

PATTY ANN. Put a sock in it, Joe, for Pete's sake.

REX. We give the money to John. You buy the house. You transfer to us. Then John gives your share to you. Fifteen hundred for your help, no strings attached.

PATTY ANN. *(to* **REX***)* Well good.

LUCY.*(to* **PATTY ANN***)* We hope you'll agree. The last time–. The children were terrified –

REX. When the landlord found out he thought it'd be best if we. Didn't stay. But this time we'll own. You can't imagine how happy we are that, how much this would mean. If you were to say yes.

(**JOE** *starts to speak,* **PATTY ANN** *cuts him off.)*

PATTY ANN. Joe and me'll talk it over of course.

REX. Of course.

(**JOE** *raises his glass.)*

JOE. But, to friends.

REX. To friends.

JOE. Fast friends.

LUCY. Yes.

(All raise their glasses.)

PATTY ANN. Of course.

(Wind, soft.)

(The yard. The present.)

(HANNAH and her husband, RICH, sit, look out.)

(The sound of kids playing as before. HANNAH holds a piece of paper and an opened envelope.)

(RICH yells out.)

RICH. That's it, that's it.

HANNAH. Rich –

RICH. Up to the top...to the *top* –

HANNAH. Don't encourage him to break his neck.

RICH. He's fine. *(calling out)* Keep going, keep –

(RICH stops, looks out into the distance, watches his son.)

RICH. See? He made it.

HANNAH. *You're* the one driving to the ER this time.

(HANNAH looks down at the piece of paper.)

(RICH looks at HANNAH looking at the paper.)

RICH. It's nothing.

HANNAH. She must have left it right after we left for school.

RICH. She's a crazy old lady, Han. It's not even typed.

HANNAH. Two weeks notice or she's seeking legal council. She actually believes she *owns* this place neither of them ever, ever said anything about the Donovan's buying this house.

RICH. The Donovans don't have a leg to stand on.

HANNAH. I should have gone over it all with them before they –. I can't believe we can't find that title in all their papers.

RICH. And they left more than their share, Hannah. Who saves old grocery bills? Old post office receipts?

HANNAH. Grandma Lucy used to wink and say "just so they know we were here". It's creepy, Mrs. Donovan leaving notes.

RICH. It's *nothing* which is why – *(calling out as before)* That's right. That's right. *Again. (to* **HANNAH***)* I'm thinking football. Pop Warner Football. Get out his aggression. That's all he needs. I did Pop Warner and I turned out fine.

HANNAH. *You* didn't bite people.

RICH. In football, there's helmets. You can't bite anybody wearing a helmet. We could make him wear it to school.

HANNAH. The teacher calls him sport.

RICH. See, they like him. He's likeable.

HANNAH. He *bites*. That's the last thing he needs to do around these people.

(The sound of children playing rises.)

RICH. *(calling out)* Oh, *oh*, wait, don't, *wait: don't* –

(Both **HANNAH** *and* **RICH** *look out, cringe.)*

RICH. Jesus.

HANNAH. *(Calling out)* Sorry. He didn't mean it. *(To* **RICH***)* Maybe you oughta –

RICH. Naw, naw, that other kid's fine. That's what boys do, they – *(calling out) Miles*. Now that's enough, Miles, that's –

*(***RICH** *and* **HANNAH** *look out.)*

HANNAH. I don't like that he is the only black kid in that class and they don't use his *name*. I see it. I see how they are with him. And I sit in those horrible meetings *which* they call us in for like my family is *new* in this town. Like we just stepped out of one of those first time home buyer's commercials where we're so happy our kids are riding bikes on cul de sacs and we have alarm systems that we don't mind if our kids' teachers

don't call our kids by their *names* cause we're too
happy we're not getting shot.
They still want to move him to another classroom.
I think they should test him again.

RICH. No more doctors. He doesn't need doctors, he just
needs time. New house, new school, it's been. Rough
for a kid.

(HANNAH *wags her head.*)

HANNAH. I know this town –

RICH. Pop Warner, you'll see.

HANNAH. I'm gonna lose it, Rich, I am, if those teachers
drag me in to one more meeting –

RICH. Next time we go in there and say "*You're* the teachers,
do your job and help us help our son."

HANNAH. You're going into logical-I-am-an-engineer-land.

RICH. Their job is to get him out of the fourth grade, not
sing Kumbaya. Next meeting we say if you can't find a
way to help this kid we're gonna send him home with
each one of you for dinner til you do and he can bite
the teacher, the principal, and each and every finger
off each and every member of that stuck up school
committee one by one til we get some answers we can
use up in here. He can bite em off, I'll grill em up
myself. With sauce.

HANNAH. You're a hot mess. This is not funny, Rich. I'm
serious.

RICH. Come here, you.

HANNAH. No.

RICH. Come here, you.

HANNAH. No.

RICH. Just come here.

(HANNAH *looks at* RICII. *Finally she crosses to him.*
RICH *looks at her.* HANNAH *looks at* RICH. RICH *tickles*
HANNAH *and* HANNAH *laughs, then tries to bat him*
away from her.)

HANNAH. See, see Stop. This is. They could have lawyers all over this already.

RICH. The Donovans don't care if our kid bites.

HANNAH. All this time I thought the Donovans were my grandparents first friends here. But instead –. Maybe that's it, maybe they made this whole thing up because they don't think we're fit for this town.

RICH. The American dollar makes you fit for this town, not the magic wand of the Donovans. Lou from Accounting is trying to buy on Mt. Vernon four hundred thousand dollars and the place needs a new roof. We're lucky.

HANNAH. I can't believe I invited them to her picnic.

RICH. What's Nessa say?

HANNAH. Well with Nessa it's a hypothetical cause she wouldn't have to move anywhere –

RICH. We are not *moving* anywhere. What happened to the old you, the warrior you, the girl I met working the door of that party who was so fierce she wouldn't let me in –

HANNAH. The cover was five dollars. Did you have five dollars?

RICH. No, I got your number instead. That girl lit the world on *fire.*

HANNAH. That girl works in Human Resources now for the flex time.

RICH. It's a job, Han, it doesn't define –

HANNAH. That girl had two kids in two years and can't even read a magazine article without thinking of grocery lists and summer camp forms. That girl moved to Leave It To Beaver's neighborhood when she should have stayed where there's decent Chinese Food.

RICH. Hey. Those are very beautiful kids: spitting image of their father. And your grandparents needed us.

HANNAH. They are. Beautiful kids. I just didn't think living here, having them would–.

RICH. *Fi-ire.*

HANNAH. Something really doesn't feel right about this Donovan thing, Rich.

RICH. Nothing is wrong.

HANNAH. Something is, Rich, something –.

RICH. If you're so tangled up about all this, call your mother, ask what she knows about any of it.

HANNAH. If two white people bought this house *for* my grandparents – the very noble and very proud Dr. and Mrs. Taylor? my mother would have gotten a bullhorn and yelled it out the front door just to spite her parents. Then she would have written a book about it. No, *if* this is true, obviously my grandparents didn't want any of us to know about it. It'd be one more reason for my mother to hate this house. She'd be glad if Nessa and I gave up this house.

RICH. You can still do it.

HANNAH. I like the quiet here. That's the one thing. My mother talks trash about this place but you can't deny there's a, something pulls me, something –

(Soft wind.)

(The sound of buttons being poured out onto a hard surface as the stage darkens and flashlight light can be seen in the yard.)

(Sounds of whispering.)

PATTY ANN. If those Vitello's wake up, Joe, we'll be the laughing stock of St. Agnes Parish.

JOE. Shhh. I just want to get one last peek.

(Bump.)

(A dog barks far off.)

(JOE walks further into the yard.)

PATTY ANN. That's it, that's – *Joe.*

JOE. The Vitellos have already moved out.

PATTY ANN. *JOE.*

> *(More barking.)*

JOE. Come here.

> *(Both stop, stand still.)*

> *(The barking stops.)*

> *(Both walk deeper into the yard.* **JOE** *stops, breathes in, satisfied.)*

JOE. Ahhh.

PATTY ANN. I don't know why I let you drag me out here.

JOE. 'Cause I've got charm you can't resist, that's why.

PATTY ANN. I need charm like a hole in the head. You told me we were going to the fancy place 'cross the Turnpike. You told me you borrowed Jimmy Greeley's car to take me out to the fancy place 'cross the Turnpike, not lurk around up here in the dark.

JOE. You can see clear across the field from here. All the way to Boston.

PATTY ANN. Well la dee da for little Mary Vitello. *(remembering)* DiMatteo that was her maiden name, remember? DiMatteo. First communion, confirmation, we did all that the same time, me and her, but I never much talked –

JOE. You can see clear and the air –

PATTY ANN. Even in school. Even in school, I never much talked to any –. Now we don't even nod hello in church. And I've known her since I was six. I was thinking about it the other day. Me and Mary Vitello were kids together, on the same street together but I don't even know the last time we spoke out loud to each other before the other day. When I think about it.

> *(***JOE*** *breathes in deeply.)*

JOE. You don't get air like this down closer to the Avenue.

PATTY ANN. Those Italians, they don't mix well.

JOE. You don't get air like this over in East.

PATTY ANN. I think it's the vines.

JOE. The what now?

PATTY ANN. The vines. You know. In their backyards.

JOE. Patty I wouldn't've brought you out here if I thought it'd have you speaking in tongues.

PATTY ANN. They have the vines, the grapevines in their backyards and I think it adds, like a mysteriousness, you know? Like they can hide back here –

(JOE *bumps into something again.*)

PATTY ANN. *Joe.*

JOE. Like thieves in the night we are.

PATTY ANN. Be careful.

JOE. I can't imagine –

PATTY ANN. We'll be the laughing stock.

JOE. – looking at houses, at where you're going to bring your wife and family, in the dead of night.

PATTY ANN. Sneaky, the more I think about it.

JOE. You don't have to like change, but to make a man root around in the dark for his family –

PATTY ANN. The wife doesn't like us.

JOE. "The wife." She has a name.

PATTY ANN. Lucy. Lucy, the wife, she doesn't –

JOE. What's not to like?

PATTY ANN. "I don't know how I'd manage." As if six babies means I'm a cow.

JOE. She never said you were a cow.

PATTY ANN. She may as well.

JOE. But she didn't.

PATTY ANN. They've got awfully long noses.

JOE. The coloreds don't have long noses.

PATTY ANN. They look down at us, that's what I mean.

JOE. Well good, because I'd have to argue with you about their noses.

PATTY ANN. Don't be an ass, Joe.

JOE. No, no, I've read all about the tribes and the way they used to be and such.

PATTY ANN. Can we go home now? We saw all this when we made a big show so the neighbors would get a good drift.

JOE. I just. Want to see. What it might be like. If it was us had to go rooting around in the dark. Tough row to hoe, Patty, tough row –

PATTY ANN. Don't you talk to me about *their* tough rows.

JOE. We're just in a hole is all.

PATTY ANN. Yeah.

JOE. We sign, we help the Taylors, and we'll be half way out –

PATTY ANN. *(sarcastic)* Half way, I should thank my lucky stars. We're all the way in a hole, Joe. I can get the electric company and the telephone company and the green grocer to tell you all about it if you don't believe me.

JOE. Just bat those pretty blue eyes at that green grocer and he won't know what hit him.

PATTY ANN. *(highly annoyed)* Aww Joe –

JOE. Oh, don't start now.

PATTY ANN. Who's starting? *(pause)* You should have told John tell the Taylor's more.

JOE. We're lucky –

PATTY ANN. We are not.

JOE. A man dreams big and he pays, Patty Ann.

PATTY ANN. The kids haven't seen new shoes in three years, Mr. Big Talk, so don't tell me about paying. We're all paying, over and over.

JOE. You, you married a dreamer.

PATTY ANN. My sister told me it should have been David O'Mahoney.

JOE. David O'Mahoney. *Bah.*

PATTY ANN. My sister told me it should have been anyone but you.

JOE. Anyone but me. Now you imagine how that makes a man feel, *Mrs. Big* Talk.

(**PATTY ANN** *and* **JOE** *look at one another.*)

(**JOE** *smiles at* **PATTY ANN**.)

(**PATTY ANN** *breaks into a smile back.*)

(**JOE** *walks to her, holds her, happy.*)

(*Soft wind.*)

PATTY ANN. It's not enough, what they're giving us.

JOE. It is. It's a lot.

PATTY ANN. Don't be so Irish about this Joe and ask for more. Fifteen hundred is not enough if there's trouble. After I found out that was them in Newton, I've done some asking around.

JOE. You shouldn't be doing that.

PATTY ANN. There's a family in the south went to jail for this kind of thing.

JOE. That was the South.

PATTY ANN. We can't go into this blind as sewer rats.

JOE. There's not sup*pos*ed to be asking around. These people get wind of the Taylors' moving truck before it pulls up and, and, well I couldn't have that on my conscience, Patty, I couldn't.

PATTY ANN. I was careful. You think I want this to fall apart? I can't take in any more washing.

JOE. I hate hearing about that washing –

PATTY ANN. Well you'll be hearing a lot more about it if we don't get enough –

JOE. This town's small. People talk.

PATTY ANN. They do exactly. How's it going to look? Us taking little handouts from people like the Taylor's? Cause once they move in, Joe, if there's talk it'll be all about how we got taken by a coupla –

JOE. How's it gonna look asking for *more* from people like the Taylor's? *That* would make us the laughing stock –.

PATTY ANN. Listen to me now because of us those girls get to move into a house our own girls'll be lucky to get a job scrubbing at the rate we're going –

JOE. That isn't nice to say.

PATTY ANN. Ask for more. Before you sign. Ask for –

JOE. We're lucky to get even this –

PATTY ANN. We are *not.* We are not, we are not. After borrowing for the fruit stand –

JOE. The world can be a grey place, Patty, I was bringing sunshine to the entire world –

PATTY ANN. And the pet store.

JOE. Who doesn't love a pet?

PATTY ANN. And the Laundromat–

JOE. Nothing like sitting and watching the clothes go 'round.

PATTY ANN. We are not lucky. Books filled with chicken scratch –

JOE. I'm a business man, I keep the real important stuff all up here *(taps his head).*

PATTY ANN. Some good "up there" did. A business man doesn't run a business stuffing his head. He works. He doesn't just dream –

JOE. I work.

PATTY ANN. Then what are we doing here then? Getting one last look at a house we could never never have. That Mary Vitello sure puts on airs for someone who grew up same as I did. She comes from the same place I did. And she's going on and on about how long it takes to clean the *down*stairs and how long it takes to clean the *up*stairs and did I see the *molding* and did I see the *trim* and did I notice there's a den and did

I notice all the trees? Because it's actually silly we sat in the Taylor's living room practically begging, teetering, *nervous* that a woman like Mrs. Taylor might not like us? A woman like that should be hoping we like *her*.

(**JOE** *goes to protest.*)

It's nothing personal, it's just the way things are supposed to be, Joe. Sitting in her living room drinking out of that woman's Waterford crystal is not the way things are supposed to be. Ask for more.

(*Beat.*)

(*The sound of crickets, soft night wind.*)

JOE. *(more to himself)* You ever just. Things slip through my fingers, because life just –

PATTY ANN. I'm tired of telling our kids no, Joe. No new shoes, no new house, no new anything because their father –

JOE. I can't punch in and punch out like the David O'Mahoneys, Patty, you know that.

PATTY ANN. Yeah, I know it.

(**JOE** *looks at* **PATTY ANN.** **PATTY ANN** *looks at* **JOE.**)

JOE. I'll go see John again –

PATTY ANN. Good.

JOE. Or maybe, maybe I go see Dr. Taylor man to man. But you stop talking about it around town. For their sake *and* for ours you stop –

PATTY ANN. *Okay.*

(*The wind blows, a bit stronger.*)

JOE. *(hopeful)* This really is our second chance, Patty.

(**PATTY ANN** *softens, smiles.*)

PATTY ANN. It is, Joe. It really is.

(*Wind.*)

(**REX** *and* **LUCY**'s *living room in the South End.*)

(The room is filled with moving boxes.)

(LUCY's hair is up in a kerchief and she wears slacks the way a woman who only wears slacks to pack or clean wears slacks.)

(LUCY looks around the room. She seems overwhelmed.)

(A great banging is heard from offstage, but LUCY doesn't move as she surveys the damage that is her living room.)

(REX enters, more moving boxes, collapsed, under each arm.)

REX. I don't think there's an empty box left in Boston.

(LUCY does not move.)

REX. But this should do it.

(LUCY does not move.)

REX. Hello? The martians have landed, they want you to report to their space ship immediately.

(LUCY does not move. LUCY bats at REX, but continues her gaze.)

REX. It's awful quiet around here. Where are the girls?

LUCY. It's bad luck.

(A bang, girls' laughter.)

REX. Ah, yes, there they are.

LUCY. Packing like this, before they sign.

REX. They'll sign.

LUCY. The wife doesn't like us.

REX. Patty.

LUCY. Patty Ann.

REX. She doesn't need to like us.

LUCY. Did you see how she looked at those glasses? Like she was inspecting them. Like they weren't good enough because they aren't Waterford or something; as if she's one of those white lace ones.

REX. Lucy –

LUCY. Rose Kennedy she's not, Rex –

REX. John wouldn't have set this up if it was bad luck.

LUCY. The *packing*. The *Packing* is bad luck. And so was bringing up the cash out in the open like that.

REX. And bringing up Newton over and over wasn't?

LUCY. That's different.

REX. There's nothing to worry about. John knows them.

LUCY. How well does he know them?

REX. They need the money. They need this just as much as we –

(*Crash.*)

REX. (*yelling off*) We're trying to take things *with us*, not break them apart.

TWO YOUNG GIRLS' VOICES. (*off, and a little less angelic than before*) We *know*.

REX. Listen to that.

LUCY. Cheeky.

REX. (*yelling off*) CHEEKY. (*to* **LUCY**) And we haven't even moved out there yet.

LUCY. Can you imagine after a year?

REX. They're not too old to take across my knee. They don't get that from me.

LUCY. *Tuh.*

REX. Their mother's a hard headed woman.

LUCY. I want to meet this John fellow. Invite him over for drinks.

REX. You don't invite a guy like John for drinks.

LUCY. Why not? Is there something the *matter* with him?

REX. There's nothing the matter with him.

LUCY. Up and up?

REX. Would I be traipsing all over the South End of Boston, looking for boxes if I thought he wasn't?

LUCY. I still don't like it.

REX. The movers are coming tomorrow.

LUCY. That doesn't mean anything. The movers came last time.

REX. You honestly believe I would trust John if something could go wrong?

LUCY. I don't want to put the girls –

REX. *(a rise of harshness) The girls are fine.*

(**LUCY** *looks at* **REX.**)

(**REX** *looks at* **LUCY.**)

LUCY. Okay, it's me. Me, *I*, don't want to go through that again.

REX. We've spent the last two years since Newton saving and planning – *together*, I might add –

LUCY. I know that.

REX. I think sometimes you forget.

LUCY. It's *our* money. Daddy gave that land to both of us –

REX. So when we sold that land and saved what we got for that land that –

LUCY. I'm not touched in the head, Rex, I know that. It's that maybe I've decided. That I like it here.

REX. Living side by side with the "unwashed", you like it here?

LUCY. Oh, I used that term as a joke. After I found that nice elderly gentleman going through our rubbish in the middle of the night –

REX. I'd lose half my patients if they knew my wife calls them names. That old man's harmless and you know it.

LUCY. I think maybe I do: like it here very much.

REX. You can't stand it here. Stacked up like pancakes, you say all the time.

LUCY. Rex –

REX. We are moving.

LUCY. *Rex –*

REX. We are moving to a beautiful house in a beautiful neighborhood in a beautiful town where we will have a beautiful yard that stretches into a field that smells like grass and earth, not concrete; where we do not have to live between four other families, where we do not have to climb two sets of stairs to put our feet up. We are doing what the rest of the country does everyday. Things are working out. I made sure.

LUCY. We should have gone through the League.

REX. I don't want our new neighbors in our business and I don't want the Bipsies and the Mopsies in it either.

LUCY. You forgot cottontail.

REX. There's nothing worse than Negroes with money.

LUCY. And Bipsy Williams would have been willing –

REX. John is willing. No cottontails allowed.

LUCY. You mock, but I think we should have stayed with our own kind –

REX. We did that last time. We had our own kind handle everything and it's no wonder we didn't last one night, none of those people probably kept their mouth shut two days about the Taylors' "big move".

LUCY. I want to meet this John, this middle man.

REX. You wouldn't like him.

LUCY. I like everyone.

REX. Is that so?

LUCY. Yes it's so.

REX. *Tuh.*

LUCY. I think I need a drink. You're giving me a headache.

REX. The bar's packed.

LUCY. That's the last thing to be packed. I think I *would* like this John. But you're trying to keep me from him. You're acting like *my* name is Bipsy.

REX. Maybe just your middle name.

LUCY. I want to ask him a few things, such as, where did you meet–?

REX. *I* can answer that –

LUCY. – How did you become acquainted?

REX. A patient. A patient knew him and knew about Newton and, and so there you have it.

(**LUCY** *looks at* **REX**.)

REX. He isn't your kind of person.

LUCY. I am not Emily Post, Rex, I simply feel there are certain ways, certain appropriate ways, to conduct oneself –

(*The girls squeal, off.*)

REX. I bet they haven't packed one thing.

LUCY. What happened to taking them across your *knee?*

(**REX** *looks at* **LUCY**. *playfully:*)

REX. You're the one I'm gonna take across my knee if you don't start helping me pack up this apartment.

LUCY. *(coy)* I'd like to see you try.

(**REX** *grins.*)

(*Beat.*)

(**LUCY** *smiles.*)

(**LUCY** *and* **REX** *embrace, kiss.*)

(*Beat.*)

(**LUCY** *plays with* **REX**'*s collar, jacket.*)

LUCY. What is this fellow John?

(**REX** *looks at* **LUCY**.)

REX. I don't know.

LUCY. Take a guess.

(**REX** *steps away.*)

REX. I don't want to.

LUCY. Take a guess.

REX. Does it matter?

LUCY. Does it matter? This is Boston, of course it matters, it always matters. Do it.

REX. ...I don't know.

LUCY. I know when you lie.

(LUCY *looks at* REX.)

REX. Portuguese.

LUCY. "John" doesn't sound Portuguese.

REX. You asked, that's what he is.

LUCY. Well see, right there, I would be worried.

REX. He isn't. It's his dad.

LUCY. They marry each other. So his dad is, his mother is, and he is.

REX. The Portuguese aren't bad.

LUCY. When I think of all those ships, I don't think they're that good.

REX. Oh here we go.

LUCY. I read, Rex. You may not anymore, but I –

REX. If I knew those books would come back to haunt me I would never have allowed you to go back.

LUCY. I didn't go back. It was one or two classes before the girls were born.

REX. Whatever it was, it was too much.

LUCY. These things get passed down, Rex, these attitudes –

REX. You're going to blame John down at Atlantic Construction Company –

LUCY. There's a history, a legacy. I wish you'd've let Daddy take you on instead of doing business with people like this.

REX. "A Negro doctor is better for show than for practicality."

LUCY. He doesn't mean that.

REX. He shouts it.

LUCY. He's in business, that's all he means. And he thinks that's more stable than collecting fees from sick patients, that's all he –. If he took you on he'd give you a fair share –

REX. I do not want him to *give* me anything.

LUCY. You sure took that land in a red hot minute.

(**REX** *looks at* **LUCY**.)

(**REX** *boils.* **REX** *calms.*)

REX. That is not the same. And John at Atlantic Construction who is helping us buy a *house*, who is helping us live like we both went to *college*, when every bank we tried promptly showed us the door –

LUCY. We didn't need those banks after all, we saved.

REX. –when every real estate office we walked into said "There? Oh, I'm afraid there's just nothing available *there*, "Doctor" Taylor".

LUCY. Why do you keep speaking to me as if you kept me in a little glass case?

REX. John down at Atlantic Construction is not responsible for the slave trade.

LUCY. Well how can I know if you won't let me talk to him? If the Donovans are agreeing why do they even need to talk to him, why don't they just come back and talk to us?

(**REX** *looks at* **LUCY**.)

LUCY. Is there a *reason*, they won't come talk to us? Rex?

(**REX** *looks at* **LUCY**. **REX** *considers.*)

REX. John. Says they'd prefer –

LUCY. The *wife* would prefer. I knew something–. That John character has all our money, Rex.

REX. I know that –

LUCY. He's got all our money while they change things around.

REX. John says Mrs. Donovan needs some convincing, that's what Mr. Donovan told him.

LUCY. No. No, no. no.

REX. But John says this is good. Not so rushed. It won't look so suspicious.

LUCY. And then we live in "their" house until that woman decides we're good enough to stay? Well I can't agree to what that woman would *prefer* –

REX. The point is they are signing.

LUCY. The martians have landed alright. They've landed and taken your brain.

REX. Less than a day after sitting up here drinking our liquor they called John even though neither of them have probably ever said more than boo to a colored man in their lives, because they're willing to play, they are willing to help. They've got barely two dimes to rub together and they are signing because they barely have a choice.

(Mischievous laughter off.)

REX. *Do not make me come in there I will not be nice.*

LUCY. They're vexed. They know it's bad luck.

REX. They are not *"vexed"* they are spoiled. Because you keep them cooped up and then ignore them –

LUCY. They are not street urchins and I give plenty of myself –

REX. I would have given anything to move to a house like that. I grew up three to a bed –

LUCY. *I know that.*

REX. They're in there breaking things, hard earned things; I work hard just to see things destroyed while their mother goes around using words that annoy people. We are moving tomorrow and we are going to like it, we are going to love it. We are going to love the space and we are going to love the air and we are going to love not having to hear every little move our children make because they will have their own rooms far away from us and I don't want to hear another word about signing or money. Period. End of discussion. Keep packing. *(very slight beat)* These boxes ought to be enough. They're coming at nine.

(**LUCY** *looks at* **REX**.)

(**REX** *looks at* **LUCY**.)

(Wind.)

(Lights rise to half on **NESSA** *and* **HANNAH**, *passing a joint back and forth as they sit on the picnic table.)*

(Each smokes, laughs.)

(An overstuffed envelope sits between them.)

HANNAH. Can you believe this shit?

MILES. *(off)* Mom?

(**HANNAH** *and* **NESSA** *extinguish and hide the joint as:)*

HANNAH. *(yelling to the house, over her shoulder)* Go ask your father.

(**HANNAH** *and* **NESSA** *wave their hands to clear the air.)*

NESSA. Fucking registered mail?

HANNAH. I can't believe this shit. Pages and pages of apartment listings all crammed into envelopes, all sitting on my front porch.

NESSA. Should we call the police?

HANNAH. "Oh, hI Bellington PD, we want you to investigate these little-old-lady notes" but, hold up, we don't know if we even own this house so maybe this old mothy white couple is right".

NESSA. They aren't.

HANNAH. Without that title we don't have any more proof than they do. She must have gotten one of her grandkids to help her, some of them are from Craigslist I know that lady doesn't know how to use Craigslist. I hope it wasn't the husband. I always liked the husband.

NESSA. What's the note say?

HANNAH. "No more borrowing, this is to help you as you go on your way".

NESSA. Jesus.

HANNAH. I always thought the husband was sweet.

NESSA. Sweet my ass, these people want us out on the street, Han.

HANNAH. Between Mrs. Donovan and that school They should give me a parking space I'm at that school so much. You should have seen that other kid, Nessa. It wasn't so much that that other kid was hurt, it was his eyes. That other kid's eyes were so frightened. Like Miles was some animal I tricked everyone into thinking was kind and sweet but when I let it run around it turns on everyone. Like if you have a hamster and you let it out and it crawls up someone's sleeve and the person's left with this *rodent* in their clothes next to their skin.

NESSA. Well shit, Han, I'd be frightened too if I asked for a crayon and someone tried to shove the whole damn box of Crayolas down my throat.

HANNAH. It's not funny.

NESSA. One day it will be.

HANNAH. He could have choked that kid to death.

NESSA. On Burnt Sienna and Indian Red?

HANNAH. They gave it a new name. It's Chestnut now. You're not allowed to call it Indian Red now.

NESSA. I used to make up stories about Indian Red.

HANNAH. That other kid was terrified.

NESSA. I used to take the pillows from the sofa –

HANNAH. I remember.

NESSA. – and box myself in and pretend I was in a canoe, my own canoe, on a river, a long, wide river with lily pads and fish only at the bottom not close cause you know how I feel about seeing them swim around near me –

HANNAH. Yeah.

NESSA. – and I was a maiden, an Indian maiden –

HANNAH. Indigenous.

NESSA. Sure.

HANNAH. No, you should say Indigenous.

NESSA. I was like *seven.*

HANNAH. Now, you should say Indigenous now.

NESSA. I was an Indian maiden. Not an Indigenous maiden. That doesn't even sound right "indigenous maiden."

HANNAH. You can take the girl out of Bellington –

NESSA. Don't compare me to these people. We got parked here when our parents were too busy to buy their own houses, make their own homes. We, we're from nowhere. Like secret agents.

HANNAH. Say Indigenous.

NESSA. I was an Indian maiden.

HANNAH. Say Indigenous.

NESSA. *I was an Indian maiden.*

HANNAH. Say Indigen –

    *(***NESSA*** jabs ***HANNAH****.)*

    (Reflexively, **HANNAH** *swats* **NESSA** *gently on the cheek. Reflexively* **NESSA** *swats* **HANNAH** *on the cheek. An old game. They hug fiercely, pull away, quiet…)*

HANNAH. Thanks for this afternoon.

NESSA. You're welcome.

HANNAH. I hate when Lucy J misses classes. I'm always. Miles takes so much –. I just wasn't sure how long they'd have me stay. And Irish Step's her favorite.

NESSA. I would have killed to take Irish Step.

HANNAH. They let anyone take it now. It's great.

NESSA. For you or the actual Irish people whose dances those are?

HANNAH. Fire that thing up again.

NESSA. I don't think so, you're all Manic Monday on me.

HANNAH. Don't torture me. I never get to. I never get to *relax.* I never even sleep anymore because there's like always this like buzzing. This, this the alarms goes off and I can't hit snooze, I haven't hit snooze in ten *years* so I wake up, wake the kids up, wake Rich up, make breakfast, make lunch, pack lunch, drive to school, drive to work, sit at work, wish I weren't at work, get off work, pick the kids up, pick dinner up, feed the kids, do homework with the kids, do violin with the kids – and they're getting better but I still have to bite the insides of my cheeks cause of that eee – eee – eee – then I put the kids to bed, argue with the kids when they are supposed to be in bed but get out of bed, wish *I* were in my *own* bed, find the perfect time between bedtime reading and teeth brushing to cram one of those beautiful orange cupcakes that I keep on top of the fridge into my mouth before one of the kids sees and Lucy J almost always sees she's got eyes like a snake that one, then return one of those beautiful orange cupcakes when I say to myself really what kind of dinner is this for a grown woman who knows to eat better so I have a fudgecicle instead because that's kind of dairy cause I'm worried about my bones, I'm worried about calcium, and do I take the right multivitamins do the Donovan's take the right multivitamins is that why they've all of a sudden come out of the wood work? Like maybe a little St. John's Wort or vitamin B or something could make them calm down about this house stuff cause I think it's just them, I hope it's just them, a lawyer would have called us if it wasn't just them and then I wonder maybe one of their grandkids is a lawyer, like some bratty kid thinks he could make a ton off this place but maybe the Donovans would chill out about all this stuff, if they only had the right multivitamins which makes me think about Rich and *his* multivitamins, and so then I wonder where *is* Rich? How does Rich escape bed time each of these nights but that's not fair to Rich I love Rich so I wonder, I wonder if Rich and I will

have sex, I wonder, if Rich and I are going to have sex
should I go shave my legs for this sex, realize Rich and
I are not going to have sex, then go to sleep and do it
all over again buzz, buzz –

NESSA. *(as she gets out the joint)* Okay, fine you know, next
time you can just ask for more smokey smoke instead
of letting your head spin around like you're possessed
Jesus.

(HANNAH is amused by her tactic.)

(They smoke.)

(NESSA turns to HANNAH.)

NESSA. You and Rich don't have sex?

HANNAH. My mouth just runs. No wonder my kid has
ADHLMNOPZ. He must get it from me. We have sex.
Just not the kind where you're sweaty after, the kind
where you remember the garbage needs to go out for
trash day after. In college we used to have the former.

NESSA. You should tell me these things.

HANNAH. You have your own life. Your own young
unmarried, unkid ridden life. You can even forget
to clean the toilet for two weeks and I bet it would
be fine. Here it would smell and no one would do
anything except look at it and look at me and say "It
smells."

NESSA. You should. Invite me over, I'll clean the toilet.

HANNAH. Nessa. When was the last time you cleaned
anything?

NESSA. Hey now.

HANNAH. Besides, I should have Yankee resolve. I should
be able to handle cleaning my own toilet.

NESSA. I know make Miles clean the toilet. Since he got
kicked out of school for a week.

HANNAH. It's not his fault.

NESSA. Yeah, crayons in the fourth grade is lame, it's that
idiot teacher's fault. It is your son's fault.

HANNAH. Miles is that hamster. Let loose into this place that isn't his. After fifty years I think I still feel like I owe something to everyone here. Like, thanks for being nice to us, here's some potato salad.

NESSA. What's Rich say?

HANNAH. Sign him up for football.

NESSA. Oh hi Token, here's your helmet.

HANNAH. It's not even bad like when mom and Auntie June grew up here. Fist fights every other day. Kids throwing rocks, bottles. Not one adult even batted an eyelash. And I can't imagine having to ask strangers to buy the place you want to call home.

NESSA. *If* they did. We don't know what really happened.

HANNAH. I don't know. Rich brought up how they kept all those paid bills, old receipts. Like they were proving to, to themselves? to us? they had a life here, and I keep wondering why they'd do that. Then I think, I'm being a jerk about this school stuff. What's my son getting called sport compared to having to sneak into this town cause no one wanted you here?

HANNAH.Oh, *and* Rich says to call mom.

NESSA. *Tuh.*

HANNAH. I know.

NESSA. When do we call mom for *anything*? Mom is best when you want to boycott grapes or ruminate on the colonial-linguistic characteristics of pygmies.

(**HANNAH** *looks at* **NESSA**.)

NESSA. Can I not say pygmies, either? Fine very tiny jungle people.

(Beat.)

HANNAH. This thing with the Donovans makes me think it's not just the school it's the whole world, like how do I keep him safe from the. It's silly.

(Beat.)

NESSA. What if, what if before the Donovans do more than leave letters on the front porch we sell this place so they can't have it either.

HANNAH. You can't sell a house you might not own.

NESSA. I don't know the logistics, but when we find the title –

HANNAH. The logistics are no, no, and no. Anyway, if Grandma wanted that she'd've left it to mom and Auntie June. They'd sell it in a red hot minute.

NESSA. Just listen to me We could sell it, buy a duplex in a neighborhood that's at least *heard* of hair grease.

HANNAH. Nessa –

NESSA. And on Sundays we could make soup and eat it all together and when we're done we will all clean your toilet.

HANNAH. Nessa.

NESSA. You hate it here. If it was me, if I lived here –

HANNAH. Well you don't.

(NESSA *looks at* HANNAH.)

NESSA. It's half mine, Hannah.

HANNAH. If it's not the Donovans.

NESSA. This house is –. You always conveniently –

HANNAH. It's half yours, I *know*.

(NESSA *looks at* HANNAH.)

NESSA. So. Since it is half mine, I say, I am suggesting we sell it and you can stop obsessing about Miles and I could pay those student loans.

HANNAH. How did this turn into a way for *you* to get what *you* want?

NESSA. I'm just pointing out that we can do more than sit here and be miserable.

HANNAH. No, no, this is your way. Just because you can't spend two years out of school, in the real –

NESSA. I have three degrees I know about the real world.

HANNAH. They are in *English* you do *not*.

NESSA. I'm *saying* –

HANNAH. I can tell you how to pay your student loans: keep a real job and stop buying shoes and handbags.

NESSA. So you get to take over everything while I get nothing? You don't deserve more than me. You and Rich can –

RICH. Rich can what?

(**RICH** *appears suddenly, sniffs the air, looks to* **HANNAH** *who looks to* **NESSA.**)

(**HANNAH** *waves the air.*)

HANNAH. Dinner's probably all ready. Crock pot –

MILES. *(offstage)* MOM? *I need you to find dad to ask him what I wanted to ask you in the first place.*

(**RICH** *does not move.*)

(**HANNAH** *looks at* **NESSA.**)

(**NESSA** *looks at* **HANNAH.**)

HANNAH. Those Donovans –

RICH. Ah.

NESSA. Those buttons were a sign, Rich –

RICH. Alright me and my meticulous engineer self will go over this house with a fine- toothed comb.

HANNAH. Thanks.

RICH. Not even her old Christmas card lists will go unturned. You two might've gotten it together to start looking through again yourselves if you weren't caught up in the weeds out here –

(He waves the air.)

(**HANNAH** *gives him a look.*)

MILES. *(offstage)* MOMMMEEEEE.

RICH. *(calling back)* We're men, son. We only call mommy in our sleep.

(**RICH** *kisses* **HANNAH.** *On the forehead.*)

(NESSA regards them.)

RICH. I'll take care of this. You'll see.

(RICH points to NESSA as the instigator of the joint.)

(NESSA looks at HANNAH.)

(HANNAH looks at NESSA.)

(They go back to arguing as soon as RICH is really gone.)

NESSA. If I can't be part of this house then I do, I want to sell it.

HANNAH. Who drove to appointments and got their groceries?

NESSA. You think you *deserve* it more than me?

HANNAH. Who changed their sheets, made sure they ate meals, took their pills?

NESSA. I was here –

HANNAH. Sitting in the yard talking and laughing while I change bedpans is not the same thing.

NESSA. You were not the only one –

HANNAH. It was just me, just me taking care of every single –

NESSA. She liked air and sun, *flowers* one last time, any of those Sundays could have been her last –

HANNAH. You do not *know* what she *wanted* –

(LUCY enters.)

(She carries the jar of buttons.)

(HANNAH and NESSA both shiver, rub their arms.)

HANNAH. Where were you when she'd reach out, call out, her voice so small, not more than a whisper, asking could I please, please stay. And I said yes, I promised I'd care the same way she –. That I wouldn't let anything happen to what they worked for. Only, I. It's very hard to, harder than I thought to live here –

NESSA. We're Indian Maidens, you and me –

HANNAH. Nessa, you're a fierce black woman til you pull on your stockings and slide into your cubicle.

NESSA. That has nothing to do –

HANNAH. We will not sell this place so you can keep buying shoes and handbags –

NESSA. WHAT HANDBAGS? I HAVE TWO HANDBAGS. I HAVE TWO HANDBAGS THAT IS NOT WHY MY STUDENT LOANS ARE CLOGGING MY THROAT –

HANNAH. You ask for that raise, then talk to me about real life.

NESSA. Oh, and what's that? A kid you can't control, a husband you can't –

(HANNAH *points at* NESSA.)

HANNAH. *Don't.* Do not.

(HANNAH *looks at* NESSA.)

(NESSA *looks at* HANNAH.)

NESSA. We're supposed to be Indian Maidens, Han Together. You don't deserve one shred more of this place than me. You don't.

(JOE *enters.*)

(LUCY *looks up at him.*)

(HANNAH *goes to enter the house.*)

HANNAH. I'm starving.

(HANNAH *exits.*)

(*After a beat,* NESSA *follows.*)

JOE. I... I...

(*Wind.*)

(JOE *steps forward.* JOE *takes a seat at the picnic table as* LUCY *goes back to sorting buttons.*)

End of Act I

ACT II

(The yard as before.)

(LUCY and JOE sit. JOE inhales deeply.)

JOE. Air's so clear up here.

LUCY. We like it.

JOE. Clean.

LUCY. That it is.

(Slight beat.)

JOE. Mrs. Donovan's sorry she couldn't make it to the housewarming.

LUCY. We understand. Dr. Taylor won't be home for hours yet. I can tell him you stopped by. I'm sure you don't want to spend your entire lunch hour talking to a housewife –

(LUCY looks at JOE.)

(JOE looks at LUCY.)

(LUCY goes back to her buttons, but does not sort.)

LUCY. Is it…is it urgent?

JOE. No, no.

LUCY. That you speak with my husband? About the house

JOE. It's not urgent. And it's such a clear day. Not one April shower. And I just thought. Since the bus up the Ave goes right by our corner and it's a clear day and. I thought, I thought since we couldn't make the…and it was so nice of you to invite…I thought it'd be nice if I visited.

LUCY. I just meant it's one o'clock on a Tuesday; maybe I should see if Rex–

JOE. I must be bothering you –

(He rises.)

LUCY. No.

JOE. Tell me if I am. Mrs. Donovan tells me if I am. I'm used to being shooed.

LUCY. The girls will be home soon. My day starts up again then.

JOE. So you're settled?

LUCY. I guess you could call it that.

JOE. And it's been...quiet?

LUCY. It's simmered down to cordial.

JOE. I'm glad. That's good.

LUCY. The party helped.We could see people peeking from behind curtains at first – no welcome wagon – but Rex decided we'd throw a housewarming party and only two for sale signs are still up. I actually prayed for that doorbell to ring. We'd gotten the girls dressed up. The Coopers were the first. The wife brought a frozen Sara Lee so I know they hadn't planned on it but for some reason they. And the others must have seen them marching up the sidewalk because more came after that and, well, only two signs left so: success.

JOE. Next time, we'll be sure to make it.

(The breeze.)

*(*JOE *looks out.)*

JOE. Looks so beautiful in the light, the sunlight.

*(*LUCY *looks at* JOE.*)*

LUCY. They're thinking of building.

JOE. Building? Nonsense. It'd be a shame to ruin all this.

LUCY. More houses. Maybe a playground.

JOE. *No.*

LUCY. This is the part I like the most.

JOE. Of course you do.

LUCY. The way the field curls up to the edge of the yard.

JOE. Yes –

LUCY. I sit here in the afternoons and just look out, breathe in.

JOE. "Field curls up to the edge." I like that.

LUCY. Like this is a very old and ancient place and we're all just borrowing it for a little bit. So it doesn't matter if there's a welcome wagon. None of us is supposed to be here anyway. I like to think. All that grass and green: it's so simple but it's very delicate. If you look over it you can see clear to Boston and you realize it's so marvelously splendid it almost hurts...

JOE. You like words.

LUCY. I spend all afternoon out here.

JOE. I can tell.

LUCY. I hide the washing and the dirty breakfast dishes in one of the cabinets. And I spend all afternoon out here. Until the girls get home. Then the housework starts up again.

JOE. But in the afternoon you let this field lap up to your toes.

LUCY. ...Yes.

(LUCY *looks at* JOE.)

(JOE *smiles sheepishly.*)

(LUCY *goes back to her buttons.*)

JOE. You were right about Frost.

LUCY. Beg pardon?

JOE. The night we met at your place. Before the house –

LUCY. That's the only place we've met.

JOE. Right.

LUCY. So of course I remember when it was –

JOE. Right. Well. I just wanted you to know. It was Frost.

LUCY. I know it was Frost.

JOE. Patty isn't interested in the books. So I couldn't say then. She gets…a bit rankled when I talk about all that stuff. But you were right. It was Frost said "good fences make good neighbors."

LUCY. "Something there is that doesn't love a wall"

JOE. "That sends the frozen-ground-swell under it"

LUCY. "And spills the upper boulders in the sun"

JOE. "And makes gaps even two can pass abreast – "

(Beat.)

JOE. It's the first poem in his *North of Boston.* I borrowed it from the library. To remind myself.

LUCY. …Can I get you something to drink, Mr. Donovan?

JOE. It's Joe. Please.

LUCY. That sun gets hot out here.

JOE. Well. Sure. I could have something to drink.

LUCY. Forgive my manners. I. Should have offered –

JOE. No need for apologies among friends.

LUCY. I'll be just a moment.

(LUCY rises, goes into the house.)

(JOE sits, sees the buttons.)

(He looks at them, picks one or two up, then places them down quickly as LUCY returns with drinks in two rocks glasses.)

(JOE looks at the glasses.)

JOE. I couldn't have asked for more.

(He smiles and takes a glass, lifts it, and he and LUCY clink glasses and then drink. LUCY notices a button out of place, and places it back.)

LUCY. I do like words.

JOE. Afternoons like this, sometimes I go down to one of the colleges. One of the big ones. BU or Northeastern. I find out when the lectures are and I sit in them and I listen and pretend I've got the book plum in front of me like the rest 'em. If I'm feeling lucky, like I can get away with it 'cause no one will notice I don't belong, I raise my hand. I ask a question. Those are good afternoons.

LUCY. They don't miss you down at the site?

JOE. Site?

LUCY. The construction site, they don't–?

JOE. Oh. No. I was never one for punching in and punching out, you see. I'm only down at the sites on occasion.

LUCY. I see.

JOE. I dream.

LUCY. That isn't very easy.

JOE. No. I suppose no, it isn't.

LUCY. Maybe you could… Since you're. Free. In the days. Maybe you could actually *go* to one of those schools.

JOE. Me?

LUCY. You could go, study, surround yourself with words, and then get a job where you're happy to punch in and punch out.

JOE. Six mouths and I'm supposed to be feedin' em all.

LUCY. Stranger things have happened.

JOE. *(Waves the idea away)* They don't want a grandpa sitting next to them in those schools.

LUCY. You don't look anything like someone's grandpa, Mr. Donovan.

(JOE *smiles.*)

(LUCY *smiles.*)

JOE. My mother would have liked it.

LUCY. See.

JOE. She sent me and my brothers to the nuns for the book learning. My brothers, they weren't much for it. One lives over on Scituate Street now. Bought a house. Married a Protestant. Two kids and they're done. They can take vacations down the cape even. My other brother owns on Appleton. Uncle Sam gave them both a leg up after the war but I was too young for all that –

LUCY. By the time Rex finished school it was almost all over. We joke that we all barely had enough time to really miss him before he came back home.

JOE. Both their wives got tired of me asking them for, well, a leg up–. But I'm lucky, in my own way. I loved those nuns. I loved those books. But my father, he died – they were both practically wet behind the ears when they first came here. County Cork – and after my father died, I, well the nuns wanted me to stay and my mother wanted me to stay, but, I suppose I realized a man can't always stay even in school when he wants to. So I set out to work to help my mother. Or. At least bring in money somehow. Met Patty Ann. We stayed down in East where we could afford enough room, or as much room as possible…we didn't know it takes a long time to save, it can take so long…but the boys do fine. It's the girls I worry about. Need privacy. More than four rooms can give. But. It can take a long time to. I try to work hard. I just.

LUCY. Can't punch in.

JOE. I can punch in alright, it's the punching out I get itchin' to do too soon after.

LUCY. Well I think you should do it. Go to one of those universities and sit there and call all those words to you. You're not punching in now so it won't be like anyone's missing anything. You should do it.

JOE. I'm a Catholic, Mrs. Taylor. There wouldn't be a divorce but there'd be so much guilt my brow would be beaten to a pulp before the first set of exams.

(Beat.)

JOE. I *wonder* if good fences make good neighbors. I meet someone I want to know what's going on behind that fence.

(Very slight beat.)

(JOE *points out a button.*)

JOE. That's a nice one there.

LUCY. It's a peculiar hobby, collecting buttons.

JOE. Not so peculiar.

LUCY. I can sit here for hours with it.I'm used to quiet. Sometimes when the girls get too rambunctious I try to will quiet back into existence.

JOE. An impossible feat.

LUCY. I married…later than any of my school friends. My father almost sent *me* to the nuns.

JOE. You took your time.

LUCY. I traveled. While Rex started his practice. Rome, Paris. Places you borrow. I was very accustomed to quiet, to being able to sit and–. I spread these out and we all sit here for hours in the sun–

TWO YOUNG GIRLS VOICES. *(from within)* MOTHER?

LUCY. Then I scoop them back up when the girls comes home.

TWO YOUNG GIRLS VOICES. *(from within)* MOTHER?

LUCY. Which they are now.

(LUCY *goes to scoop up the buttons and* JOE *goes to help her. Their fingers touch.*)

(LUCY *looks at* JOE. JOE *looks at* LUCY.)

(JOE *holds* LUCY*'S hand for a beat too long.* LUCY *looks at* JOE. JOE *looks at* LUCY.)

A YOUNG GIRL'S VOICE. *(from within)* MOTHER.

(JOE *takes a step toward* LUCY.)

JOE. Something there is that wants it down. I don't often get to. Talk like this.

(JOE *looks at* LUCY. LUCY *looks at* JOE.)

(LUCY *pulls her hand away, scoops up the buttons and places them in the jar.*)

LUCY. Should I tell Dr. Taylor you stopped in?

JOE. ...No. No, I. It isn't urgent.

LUCY. Have a good afternoon, Mr. Donovan.

JOE. You as well, Mrs. Taylor.

TWO YOUNG GIRLS VOICES. *(from within) Mother.*

> (**LUCY** *holds up the last of her drink to* **JOE**. **JOE** *raises his glass, too.)*

> (**LUCY** *downs the rest of her drink in one gulp, picks up the jar, and looks to the house.)*

LUCY. Afternoons are the only part I like.

> *(She turns, heads into the house.)*

> (**JOE** *places his glass on the picnic table.)*

> *(Stillness.)*

RICH. *(off, as he storms into the yard)* No, no, no.

> (**HANNAH** *enters on his heels.)*

HANNAH. For a little while.

RICH. I don't like it. I don't want him home schooled.

HANNAH. For a little while.

RICH. And so we just, we just, have you barricade yourself up in the house –

HANNAH. It's not barricading –

RICH. I don't want to live like those Montana people.

RICH. This town has other schools, other fourth grades.

HANNAH. Who's going to take him this far into spring?

RICH. No.

HANNAH. I can take some leave –

RICH. Our kid *attacked* another kid. He needs structure –

HANNAH. I don't want him playing sports with these kids. I don't want him winning games for their parents, for schools that don't want him, for old ladies who leave notes telling us to move out of our own house.

RICH. He stuffed a box of crayons down another kid's throat, Hannah –

HANNAH. I know that.

RICH. He does not deserve a vacation with mommy, eating cookies and watching PBS all day.

HANNAH. That was just when he was on suspension. I can teach real stuff.

RICH. You took time off we couldn't afford. You are not homeschooling our son because you're afraid –

HANNAH. It's that I don't like how they *are* with him. I can't send him back, Rich, I won't everyone looking at him –

RICH. – like he's the kid who stuffed crayons down another kid's –

HANNAH. I know what he did you don't have to keep *repeating* it, like, like I did something to make him –

RICH. I'm not saying it's your fault, I'm saying your anxieties –

(RICH *looks at* HANNAH.)

(HANNAH *looks at* RICH.)

HANNAH. My anxieties? My "racial" anxieties?

RICH. Yes. Your *anxieties* about things that are racial, yes. Are getting a little.

HANNAH. I won't do it. I will not send him back.

RICH. What you think and feel. It isn't fair to place those.

HANNAH. I am not *placing* anything. How am I?

RICH. What you want to do isn't about protecting him.

HANNAH. It is. That's what a parent –

RICH. You don't want him mixing with these people.

HANNAH. Keep your voice down. I am concerned about *Miles.* I don't care about these other kids.

RICH. The school doesn't hate him. *You* hate the *school.*

HANNAH. I do not.

RICH. This is not Little Rock, Hannah.

HANNAH. I *know* that.

RICH. Miles is not some kid leading the forces of integration –

HANNAH. Don't condescend. The note, the letters, are real. Us not finding the title to this house is real. The more I think about it, the more I think, I mean a part of me *knows*...the Donovans might not be wrong.

RICH. I do not want my son home schooled because of some ridiculous demands from an old lady that are spinning your many, many problems with that teacher, that school, this town –

HANNAH. My grandfather was a doctor. My father has two PhDs. My mother had a Fulbright. That teacher treats our son like he's the first person in our family to know the goddamn alphabet. It is not in my head I am not making it up.

RICH. Miles has problems, Hannah. Maybe Miles is the first person in your family who. Has. Problems. School problems.

HANNAH. He can't afford to have school problems. He is black and this is America –

RICH. You're telling *me* what it's like to be black and male in America, Han?

HANNAH. You know what I mean.

RICH. Could I see some ID sir –

HANNAH. Rich –

RICH. Could you step out of the vehicle sir –

HANNAH. Rich, come on, you know what I –

RICH. Hands where I can see them, sir –

HANNAH. Stop it.

    (**RICH** *looks at* **HANNAH**.)

    (**RICH** *looks at* **HANNAH**.)

    (**RICH** *looks away*.)

    (*Beat.*)

    (*Beat.*)

HANNAH. I'm sorry.

    (**RICH** *looks at* **HANNAH**.)

RICH. You know what? Maybe all Miles proves is that your family is *normal*. With normal problems that you, we, need to look dead in the eye before they. He's just a kid. You can't lock him away.

(**PATTY ANN** *at an ironing board ironing.*)

(*She wipes her brow of sweat, then continues ironing. Stacks of ironing, in brown paper packaging and twine, surround her. We hear humming.* **PATTY ANN** *stops, listens, when* **JOE** *enters humming, she goes back to ironing.*)

PATTY ANN. Well?

JOE. Lovely afternoon, lovely.

PATTY ANN. What'd they say?

JOE. You've got all the kids out, playing in the air, that's wonderful –

PATTY ANN. *What'd they say?*

JOE. You'll faint of the heat stroke if you don't open a window.

PATTY ANN. You talk to them?

JOE. Dr. Taylor was not at home.

PATTY ANN. You talk to her?

JOE. I don't want to spoil a lovely afternoon, Patty.

PATTY ANN. Don't you Patty me. You Patty me when you didn't do like I said. There's an Ann in there Mr. and I hope you did what I said.

JOE. The bus isn't so bad, you know. I don't miss the car at all.

PATTY ANN. So you're going back, then. Tell them that title ain't ever gonna look any different than it does if we don't see more money.

JOE. Maybe it's best to keep a tight lid on all this, now, till the Taylor's are settled –

PATTY ANN. I should have gone myself.

JOE. I don't know if we should be bothering them.

PATTY ANN. Botherin' them. That house is ours right now, Joe.

JOE. That house was paid for by the Taylors –

PATTY ANN. You said you went down to John and told him we don't sign it over to the Taylors till we see more.

JOE. It doesn't feel right –

PATTY ANN. And you said John said any time, Joe Donovan, any time you go and see "the good doctor" and he'll see to it you get what you need.

JOE. Well maybe it wasn't said like that exactly –

PATTY ANN. Good doing business with you, Joe Donovan, is what you said John said.

(We see REX, drink in one hand, cigar in the other, in the backyard.)

JOE. I, I don't know if I remember it like that, now –

PATTY ANN. Well that's convenient.

JOE. A man's King of his own castle, Patty Ann –

PATTY ANN. Then act like it and go do what I told you to do. I'm the one being bothered, while you go traipsing up the Avenue (sniffs) smelling of drink, how can you smell of drink; it's not even four. You should be ashamed of yourself.

JOE. On the bus coming home, I had a thought.

PATTY ANN. Oh no.

JOE. What if we take a bit of the money and, and, I make a real change. A real deep honest to goodness real three hundred and sixty degree change

PATTY ANN. Three hundred and sixty did you say?

JOE. Round about and loopty loop.

PATTY ANN. …Keep talking.

JOE. On the bus up the Ave I got to thinking and I think, I think, I'm not using my talents, Patty Ann.

PATTY ANN. And by talents you mean…?

JOE. I was thinking, what I need to do is, what I need to, see, since I was little I've, you know I've loved opening up my mind –

PATTY ANN. Opening up your mouth is more like it. I've heard all about your thinking for the past fifteen years Mr. Donovan, and look where it's gotten me. Up to my ears in other people's skivvies.

JOE. I'm going to University.

(Beat.)

*(**PATTY ANN** turns to her ironing board. **PATTY ANN** picks up the iron. **PATTY ANN** shakes her head. **PATTY ANN** leans into her ironing.)*

JOE. What do you think? I'm going to be a man of letters. Just like Ma and Dad would have liked, like they got on the boat for, no breaking my back and my hands, I'm going to use my talents, my God given talents and get paid for them.

*(**PATTY ANN** irons.)*

JOE. I take a little of that money and go to one of the universities and four years from now, Patty, four years from now we get our own house; we leave the Taylors alone and we get our own house –

*(**PATTY ANN** irons.)*

JOE. I think it's a fine idea.

*(**PATTY ANN** shakes her head as she irons.)*

JOE. As I was coming up the Ave on the bus – and I don't, I don't miss the car one bit. New tires–psshhh – buying new tires won't help in the long run, this, my *plan*, will help in the long run.

(He goes to her, about to hold her.)

JOE. This will help in the long –

(As he is about to touch her, she turns, wielding the iron.)

(Steam showers **JOE** *and he jumps back.)*

PATTY ANN. Now you listen to me. *I* miss the car. *I* miss the car very *much.* I ask you to do this and you can't even... I've been doing some thinking too and that house is practically ours.

JOE. Now it's not –

(She wields the iron.)

PATTY ANN. My fingers ache, Joe. *My* back broke a long time ago and if it takes me fifty years I'll get what's coming to me because they don't deserve it. We do.

(Beat.)

*(***PATTY ANN*** lowers the iron slowly. She places the iron on the ironing board. She irons.)*

JOE. It's not right.

*(***PATTY ANN*** stops ironing, freezes.)*

JOE. I'll pick up a shift. I'll buy four new whitewalls. A man's king of his castle, now, and. The more *I* think of it, I can't have us doing that. I won't.

(Beat.)

*(***PATTY ANN*** goes back to ironing.)*

PATTY ANN. We'll see.

*(***PATTY ANN*** irons.)*

(The steam from the iron rises, rises in a way it never could have. It fills the stage and rolls into the yard like fog.)

*(***LUCY*** joins **REX** in the yard.)*

REX. You should have called me.

LUCY. The girls were practically underfoot the entire time.

REX. He didn't leave anything, say anything?

LUCY. You're acting awfully peculiar.

REX. You should have asked him to wait.

LUCY. Well how was I to know when you'd be home? It's not every night you grace us with your presence. There's always a patient, some emergency demanding your attention.

REX. Who else is going to pay for new rugs, new curtains –

LUCY. This house is four times the size –

REX. And it's a hell of a drive, Lucy all the way in to Columbus Avenue, all the way back, up the turnpike –

LUCY. I didn't come out to argue, I came out to say I laid out a shirt for tomorrow night.

REX. Joe Donovan shows up, you call. You don't leave me to find out from the girls what goes on in my own house.

LUCY. You're blowing everything out of proportion. Now, tomorrow's conference night, remember. I set out that specific shirt. I bet those teachers have never laid eyes on a Negro doctor. I want to make a superior impression.

REX. I still think it's strange Joe Donovan –

LUCY. I think it's strange you're so upset – especially since we're all settled, everything's been taken care of.

REX. He's neck deep, stuck, liable to do anything.

LUCY. Everything has been taken care of, yes?

(Pause.)

REX. Yes.

LUCY. And he seemed fine. Although it was hard to tell. The girls –

REX. The girls… It was nice to eat with them again. They're quieter than I remember.

LUCY. You wouldn't say that if you were here more.

REX. I hardly hear their voices anymore. I miss the four of us. At night, I could hear when their cover's slipped off. I could see your shoulder across the dark in the street light. Now there's so much space I can't see anything.

*(**LUCY** takes **REX** in.)*

LUCY. I'm still here.

(Beat.)

LUCY. Well, I can barely stand, I'm beyond exhausted –

REX. It's a hell of a drive, but sometimes I don't come up the Turnpike, sometimes I turn off and come through Medford, the west side of Medford. Some nice Negro families live over there. Maybe I… Because I was the only one in line for twenty minutes at the post office, before anyone waited on me. I knew it'd be difficult –

LUCY. I don't miss three families living one on top of the other, I can tell you that.

REX. Maybe I'm still that sappy kid whose mama kept all his marks in a book next to the family Bible.

LUCY. Until you brought me home you thought those pages were lined with real gold –

REX. You shouldn't have pointed that out in front of mama.

LUCY. She liked me anyway.

REX. *Tuh.*

*(**LUCY** swats playfully at him.)*

REX. I'm still that sappy kid 'cause I thought I'd lifted us, you, me, the kids, I thought I'd lifted us all up but maybe living all the way out here isn't where we're supposed to be.

LUCY. *(Matter of fact and slightly incredulous)* Wherever we are is where we're supposed to be.

*(**REX** looks at **LUCY**.)*

*(**LUCY** looks at **REX**.)*

REX. But I don't *feel* lifted. I should feel Nevermind. Go to bed.

*(**LUCY** goes to the house.)*

*(**RICH** sits bundled in a hooded college sweatshirt. It's a good school, but not an Ivy. He faces the field, a bottle*

of scotch and the glass from before by his side. It's good scotch, but not great.)

(A pile of mail sits next to him.)

(NESSA enters. She backs into the yard carefully, blanket in hand, back pack on her shoulder, and spreads the blanket on the ground, far enough away from the picnic table so that she doesn't notice RICH and is startled when he speaks.)

RICH. What's with the blanket?

(NESSA jumps.)

NESSA. *Jesus.*

RICH. Camping out?

NESSA. What are you doing up?

RICH. Liquid dreams.

(RICH holds up the bottle.)

To take the place of my *actual* dreams. Which, this evening, are determined to keep me awake until the end of time.

(RICH smiles. RICH offers the bottle to NESSA.)

(NESSA goes to take the bottle, RICH yanks playfully away, then finally offers again.)

(NESSA accepts, swigs.)

RICH. What kind of Taylor woman would you be, if you refused a drink?

(NESSA drinks, looks out.)

(She's restless.)

RICH. Really, what're you doing with all that?

NESSA. I'm surveying. Claiming what's rightfully mine.

RICH. You and Hannah are wound *tight*, let me tell you. All the degrees in this family: one of you should study up on *chill.*

NESSA. Everyone needs to start taking me seriously after we get the Donovan's off our backs. Hannah–

RICH. Hannah is checking the mirrors and keyholes for Mrs. Donovan.

NESSA. My day's been too sucky for you make fun of me.

RICH. Hannah is writing manifestos about Brown versus Topeka –

NESSA. For real.

RICH. – versus Rodney King versus Plessy versus Malcolm X and Dr. Martin Luther King Jr. walk into a bar –

NESSA. I didn't get that promotion. The Donovans want to take the only home I've known and I didn't get that promotion. I want to say it's all their fault but it's, it's probably me. Grandma Lucy, my mother, especially, taught us to be, to be on guard, you know? I used to think everyone ended up like this. After high school, after college, after your first job when the guy you started as an intern with gets promoted and you can't bond over the five dollar Indian lunch buffet cause all of a sudden he has enough to go to P.F. Chang's or something.

I didn't get that promotion, but Craig, who spends half his day tending a virtual farm on Facebook? he asked for it last week and I don't think everyone else builds a cubicle around themselves. I don't think everyone else is too afraid to ask for what they want. The whole office except me took him out to celebrate and that was all he could talk about was P.F. Changs. And sitting next to him I swore I could smell something very old on the sleeves of his shirts, on the curves of his cuffs.

RICH. Ah, yes, the smell of entitlement.

(NESSA cracks a bit, a laugh.)

RICH. P.F. Chang's sucks, Ness.

NESSA. They have these lettuce wraps that are actually very good.

RICH. I don't get it. When all "the other" folks couldn't even sit at Woolworth's and eat a hot dog your family was in like Flynn and you're *still* not happy.

NESSA. Teacher looked like you, the mailman looked like you. You always fit.

RICH. There's no ShangrI La where all the black people rejoice and sing because they can all share hair grease.

NESSA. DC Chocolate City –

RICH. *Anacostia River.* The *other* river. The one between the folks and the votes. Fifth grade, we went on a field trip. We sailed across that river and I tell you my heart nearly broke out of my chest. Why hadn't anyone told me about this world, about this place? Stone and slate and marble. Monuments everywhere you turn. You can look Lincoln in the eye. I came home and asked my father why he'd never taken me over that river, why it took ten years for me to find out about life on the other side of that river. You know what he said? "Nobody's stopping you". And nobody's kept me out of anything since. When I met Hannah she lived like that too. Italy, England, Ethiopia even, remember?...your sister'd been all over the place. She walked around like she deserved–. I could even feel it in her skin, when she sat next to–. Blew *my* little engineer mind, for The dream I keep having is I'm on this field. I've got this football helmet on and I'm running in place and I'm decked out in red and grey –

NESSA. Go Bellington!

RICH. And through the face mask I can just make out Hannah. Very far away. She can't see me. She's sitting out across a huge field and she's all alone and she won't move, she can't move, she's very still and she's very sad and she gets smaller and smaller I know I'll never see her again. I wake up in a cold sweat and not even two hours of Sportscenter can get me back to sleep.

Hannah's taking this house thing, this Miles thing... She's not right about any of it. I check the mileage in the car. She doesn't go anywhere. The groceries are coming from online now, the dry cleaning gets delivered. And I found all this mail stuffed in between the cushions of the couch.

Any mail that mentions this town, stuffed between the cushions of the couch.

(He goes through the mail.)

Town Council Meeting, Town School Board Meeting, Town paper, Mrs. Donovan- there's-nice-places-in-Cambridge, in Lexington, invite *(he opens it)* Simon Greeley's turning ten. Before I die I'd like to go to just one more party where the drinks aren't served in sippy cups.

NESSA. I knew those buttons were a sign. Everything's going to shit.

RICH. Those buttons have Hannah – you know I found her staring at one them. Came home from work, the DVD was on before dinner which she never allows never. And something was gurgling on the stove and she's just staring, staring at one of those… Why do you look like you're camping out in the middle of the night? And how come I didn't hear your car? That muffler usually announces itself.

NESSA. I parked over on Appleton. I was afraid if Hannah heard my car, knew I was here she might–. You know, she never calls me. We talk all the time, so she thinks she does, but I'm always the one to call her. And she won't listen to anything I say about this house –

RICH. *(waggin his head)* This house.

NESSA. That sounds like you know something. What'd you find? Cause as soon as we straighten out the Donovan thing we need to sit and talk, like equals. Everywhere else I'm always justifying why I deserve what I deserve and Craig may have gotten than promotion but I won't let Hannah do that to me in my own house –

RICH. "Your" own house?

NESSA. What's that mean?

RICH. Who in this world *deserves* anything, that's all I'm saying.

NESSA. If you were the one being squeezed out –

RICH. I don't want to squeeze anyone out. I don't care who it goes to. I just know, I just *know* Hannah's never gonna come out of this if she keeps spinning and spinning like you all do. This house is too tricky for it's own good.

NESSA. What's "tricky" mean?

RICH. Ghost bought.

NESSA. What are you talking about?

RICH. That's the term for it, I guess. For when black folks couldn't buy for themselves so they'd get a white family to buy for them. A white couple in Kentucky went to jail for treason back in the day. The black couple's house? firebombed.

NESSA. Jesus.

RICH. All under the table, through the back door stuff ghosts.

NESSA. So that's –. What about the title?

RICH. I'll find it.

NESSA. They could have told us. I don't understand why –

RICH. They were too proud for that.

NESSA. So the Donovan's are right.

RICH. I didn't say that, now.

NESSA. If this is all true –

(*A breeze.*)

(*We catch a glimpse of* **PATTY ANN**, *a shadow of a figure, putting on gloves.*)

(*We catch a glimpse of* **HANNAH**, *who holds up a button, regards it.*)

(*Wind.*)

(**NESSA** *takes a swig.*)

(The breeze dies down.)

(PATTY ANN *is gone.)*

NESSA. Well, *shit.*

RICH. *Chiiiilllll.*

NESSA. I don't understand I don't understand why so much is so difficult because it shouldn't be it –. When I was little and would get like this, Hannah'd, Hannah'd always be right there.

RICH. I miss her too –

*(**NESSA** and **RICH**'s eyes meet. **NESSA** steps forward, too close. Beat.)*

*(**RICH** steps away. **NESSA** steps away.)*

*(The sound of dogs barking, as before with **PATTY ANN** and* **JOE.***)*

NESSA. I shouldn't be getting my drink on while those Donovans are trying to send us back to Africa.

RICH. I don't know why you're talking about Africa all my greats and all my grands were from Barbados, mon [pronounced more Bajan than Jamaican], they can send me back *there* cause I sure as hell could use a vacation. Shit. Don't worry about this house.

NESSA. All that ease. You've got it too. Hannah's lucky.

*(**LUCY** and **PATTY ANN**, hats and gloves in place, sit at a table, cups of coffee on saucers in front of them.)*

(They sit and sip with a frosty gulf between them.)

*(Finally, **PATTY ANN** places her cup down, looks at **LUCY**. **LUCY** places her cup down, too.)*

PATTY ANN. I'm so glad you could meet with me like this.

LUCY. Well I'm glad I was available. At such short notice. Usually I have a class.

PATTY ANN. I was never one who went in for the books.

*(**LUCY** blinks.)*

PATTY ANN. My brother Sean's nose was always in a book, and the only places he's fit for now is the library and the priesthood. Thank goodness the church keeps a roof over his head. Books aren't practical if you ask me. A grown man should be able to pay for his own shoes.

(Beat.)

Now, the house.

LUCY. The house?

PATTY ANN. The Vitello's house.

LUCY. Our house.

PATTY ANN. I always had a deep admiration for the Vitellos.

LUCY. Mrs. Vitello –

PATTY ANN. Mary. That's her Christian name. We were in school together, we were girls together –

LUCY. I bought Mrs. Vitello a volume of Keats, in fact, to show how grateful the new family in their beautiful house –

PATTY ANN. I'm not sure I understand why you'd do that.

LUCY. I'm so glad you called, you can give me her new address –

PATTY ANN. I'm not sure that's a very good idea.

PATTY ANN. You should probably be discreet –

LUCY. Discreet, yes, that's the correct word.

PATTY ANN. I know how to speak.

LUCY. I'll be indubitably discreet. Use my mother's maiden name, sign it in invisible ink –

PATTY ANN. I'm not sure that's a very good idea, bringing the Vitello's back into this.

LUCY. Well with them all the way down in Florida I don't see –

PATTY ANN. I'm sure I don't have to remind you how quickly things can get ugly –

LUCY. And I don't need to remind you, I'm sure, that we put our lives at stake for that house.

PATTY ANN. Up the hill is no war zone, I'd dare say.

LUCY. You try living in the middle of so much neighborly goodness, you'd choke on all the kindness.

PATTY ANN. I'd appreciate such torture as living in that house would bring, let me tell you.

LUCY. I wouldn't be so sure.

PATTY ANN. It is a very nice house.

LUCY. It is.

PATTY ANN. In a very nice neighborhood.

LUCY. It is.

PATTY ANN. You zipped in, no problems –

LUCY. We're lucky.

PATTY ANN. Quite. Yes. And that's why I rang for you to meet me.

LUCY. Doctor Taylor takes care of these types of things. Perhaps you should have rung for him, not me. I'm not sure why this has anything to do with me at all.

PATTY ANN. You moved in no problems and get to enjoy every inch of that house.

LUCY. It's getting late.

PATTY ANN. The den, the trim, the molding –

LUCY. We should all meet the four of us –

PATTY ANN. Because of us, no problems, and I think –

LUCY. We should all meet, the four of –

PATTY ANN. I think we should take more into consider –

LUCY. And it's getting late in the day, the girls will be getting back soon –

PATTY ANN. You moved in and I think, I think we deserve –

(**LUCY** *opens her purse.*)

LUCY. I'm so sorry, but the girls… This is on me.

(*She lays down money on the table.*)

PATTY ANN. I can pay for a lousy cup of coffee.

LUCY. Can you. Have Joe talk to Doctor Taylor.

PATTY ANN. I sent Mr. Donovan to talk to your husband and he came back high on the books.

LUCY. It's a peculiar person to me who doesn't enjoy a good book.

PATTY ANN. You've got a lot of nerve sitting here talking to me like –

LUCY. Doctor Taylor takes care of these types of things. Now, if you'll excuse me, the girls –

PATTY ANN. Lucky little girls.

LUCY. Yes –

PATTY ANN. Big house up on the hill.

LUCY. Please, don't make this difficult.

PATTY ANN. I bet they each have their own room.

LUCY. Don't make this –

PATTY ANN. My girls don't have their own rooms.

LUCY. Well with the money –

PATTY ANN. Already pissed down the toilet.

LUCY. Perhaps you should lower your voice –

PATTY ANN. After all that we borrowed for the fruit stand and the pet store; after all the money owed back to his brothers so I can look their snot nosed wives in the eye stead of crossing the street if I see them on the Ave. We deserve more for getting you into this town. My girls share a bed.

LUCY. Really, pay a call on Doctor –

PATTY ANN. My girls take in mending, my girls wash and iron and don't have time for "volumes" of anything.

LUCY. You don't want them to have volumes of anything, you just said –

PATTY ANN. Your girls are borrowing our luck.

LUCY. I beg your pardon.

PATTY ANN. My girls shouldn't be mending and washing and iron –

LUCY. And my girls should.

PATTY ANN. I'm just...explaining...there is an *order* to
things. You know there's an order to things, or you
wouldn't have begged us –

LUCY. Who was begging? There was no –

PATTY ANN. There's an order to things and you know and
I know you and your girls are borrowing –

LUCY. Talk to –

PATTY ANN. And it makes me sick. To think my girls don't
have two sticks to rub together while, while –

LUCY. There's nothing more to discuss. Everything's
signed.

PATTY ANN. That title is still in our name.

LUCY. I assure you, it is *not*. Doctor Taylor wouldn't let
something like that slide.

PATTY ANN. He has too, he has too let that slide.

LUCY. Talk to Joe.

PATTY ANN. I've got more metal than to leave everything
up to my husband and you're forgetting who was here
first, in Bellington first –

LUCY. Everything's signed.

PATTY ANN. I could make it very uncomfortable for you. If
that title were to turn up different than you want.

(**LUCY** *scoffs.*)

PATTY ANN. I could. Because let's say that title didn't get
signed the way it was supposed to –

LUCY. I assure you –

PATTY ANN. And let's say I've been living here in Bellington
since I was a girl and and let's say I might not have
much but I do have this town, more than you do, and
let's say maybe I went to school with a girl or two works
down the town hall. Maybe I went to school with a girl
or two was willing to make sure I get what I deserve
to get. Which is more than what we got, I know that
much. I could make it. Very uncomfortable.

(**LUCY** *lifts her coffee cup to her lips, sips coolly.*)

PATTY ANN. Joe and me both could.

(**LUCY** *places the coffee cup on the saucer gently, lifts her napkin, and dabs her mouth.*)

LUCY. It's Joe and I and quite frankly I don't see how I can possibly help you. You can't threaten me to, to. You go on and on about your girls, your girls. You fail to understand that I don't care one pinky finger about your girls.

PATTY ANN. That's for sure –

LUCY. That little war between the states I'm sure you would have read about in school if you'd been one for the books, as you so eloquently put it, ended a very long time ago and I couldn't care less if your girls took a flying leap into the Charles River.

PATTY ANN. You've got some nerve –

LUCY. You won't push us out, if that's what you're thinking. My girls won't be pushed out just because you've *decided*, just because you *say*. This town that you think is going to come to your aid, you can't even walk its streets like a decent–. My girls belong here just as much as each of yours. No, they won't be pushed, I won't let that happen and you can count on every last finger and toe I will not, not ever, let that happen. Now, I suggest you talk to *Doctor* Taylor. Or have Joe talk to Doctor Taylor. He's the one who handles these things. I can't possibly help you.

(**LUCY** *stands.*)

Now I don't want the girls coming home to an empty house.

(*Patting the money she's left on the table.*)

This should be enough for us both. I know times are hard. You have a good afternoon.

(*We see **PATTY ANN**'s shoulders rise and fall in anger and indignation, again and again.*)

*(We see **PATTY ANN** remove a sheet of paper from her purse.)*

*(**PATTY ANN**'s shoulders rise and fall, rise and fall. The paper trembles in her hands as the lights lower on her.)*

(The sound of many buttons.)

*(**HANNAH** stands at the picnic table, examines one button, then another.)*

*(**LUCY** shifts, still in same clothing as in the diner, but she is excited, exuberant.)*

*(**LUCY** and **REX** in their yard.)*

REX. …You shouldn't be *meeting* alone with these people in the first place Lucy, end of story. Find something else to do besides meddle –

LUCY. Protecting our house, our home, is meddling?

REX. She calls you, you call me. He visits here, you –

LUCY. I want to see that title.

REX. John –

LUCY. Our name on that title I want to see it, if everything's been handled, if everything is fine and taken care of.

*(**REX** looks at **LUCY**.)*

LUCY. Right now.

REX. …All this pulling on of armor, this getting ready for battle every time we leave the front door…

LUCY. We do own this house, Rex, yes?

*(**REX** looks at **LUCY**.)*

LUCY. Rex?

REX. …No.

(Silence.)

Not yet, no.

(Silence.)

If I could just talk to Joe Donovan. Me, John, we've both been trying to. If I could get a hold of him, complete

our arrangement, we, we, could sell and move to one
of those houses in Medford, West Medford –

LUCY. We didn't come all this way to *lose*. You're trying to
give up.

REX. You were right. This is bad luck.

LUCY. You're giving up and it's beneath you, it's beneath
both of us. Thick skin is what it's going to take. As long
as I have breath in my body I will show these people
what's what. Frozen Sara Lee *tuh*. You bake for your
neighbors. You use ribbon. You write a card. I won't be
pushed out. I won't have us buying another house. We
bought *this* house. That title belongs in my hand, Rex.
You're going to make this right, believe me. Those
teachers' tongues will wag if we're late. Hurry up. Go
change.

(REX *looks at* LUCY.)

(LUCY *looks at* REX.)

(*Wind.*)

(MILES *enters the yard, workbook and pencil in hand,
and* HANNAH *places the buttons in her hand back in
the jar.*)

(HANNAH *regards* MILES, *watches him attempt to work.*)

HANNAH. And this one?

MILES. I think I heard the ice cream truck.

HANNAH. I didn't hear the ice cream truck.

MILES. I did.

HANNAH. Just finish.

MILES. Is Italian ice really from Italian?

HANNAH. Italy.

MILES. Or maybe I could get a snow cone. That's what
I want, a snow cone.

HANNAH. *Finish.*

MILES. You don't smell anything like Mrs. Granger.

HANNAH. The sooner we finish, the sooner you can go find the ice cream truck.

MILES. The smell of Mrs. Granger helps me work.

HANNAH. Miles.

MILES. It does.

HANNAH. I don't want to argue.

MILES. I can't do it like this.

HANNAH. Yes. You can.

MILES. Talk to Mrs. Granger.

HANNAH. I don't need to talk to Mrs. Granger.

MILES. She'll tell you.

HANNAH. It's taken two hours to do half a page of real work, not just drawings.

MILES. I work better at school.

HANNAH. This *is* school. Now.

MILES. No, this sucks.

HANNAH. Watch your mouth.

MILES. I think I should be doing this in *school*, not the backyard.

HANNAH. Shh and do your work.

MILES. You do it.

HANNAH. I don't need to do it, I finished school.

MILES. I miss my friends.

HANNAH. You can phone them. Besides, you'll make new friends.

MILES. Yeah, right, like *where?*

HANNAH. At the home school group –

MILES. Those kids are weirdos and I don't need new friends. I have plenty of friends. They call me "M" and think I'm cool cause I'm the only one in gym who can make lay ups no problem all the time.

HANNAH. You can do more than sports, Miles.

MILES. M.

HANNAH. Your name is *Miles*.

MILES. I'll get to see them at Simon's.

HANNAH. Simon's?

MILES. Simon Greeley's having a birthday. The invitation thing's coming in the mail.

HANNAH. Is it?

MILES. Yep. Me and Simon like to kick it old school.

HANNAH. Well, I'll keep my eye out.

MILES. Good. Cause I don't wants to disappoints my fans.

HANNAH. Where'd you learn to talk like that?

MILES. At school I'm cool.

HANNAH. Well this isn't school so speak correctly.

MILES. You just said it *was* school.

(*NESSA enters.*)

(*HANNAH takes her in.*)

MILES. HI AUNTIE NESSA.

HANNAH. *FINISH.*

NESSA. Hey Miles. Hannah.

MILES. How come you're not picking on Lucy J. like this?

HANNAH. Who's picking on you? I am asking you to do work you were supposed to do two days ago.

MILES. Pick on Lucy.

HANNAH. Work.

MILES. This is *stupid.* I belong in *school.* If I were in school I'd be done with work by now cause it's five o'clock. Why do I have to keep doing this? Cool guys don't do this crap.

HANNAH. What did I just say about language –

MILES. Cool guys –

HANNAH. Enough with the cool guys, I don't want you to be a cool guy. I don't want you to be these people's cool guy pet token black basketball playing, football toting mascot – because that's what is happening, that is what is – they call you sport and say you're cool but they aren't going to let you date their daughters, they won't let you ten feet near their front gate. I don't want you at Simon Greeley's I want you to be a human being.

(Beat.)

*(**MILES** does not move.)*

NESSA. You're really good at this homeschooling stuff.

*(**HANNAH** stops, exhales in defeat.)*

HANNAH. Maybe go find that ice cream truck.

*(**MILES** looks at her.)*

HANNAH. Go ahead. Go.

*(**MILES** looks at her. Beat. He hugs her suddenly and she relaxes.)*

*(**MILES** runs off)*

MILES. Sno cone, sno cone, sno cone, sno cone…

(The breeze.)

*(**HANNAH** picks up **MILES**' "school" work.)*

NESSA. I wrote a paper once, on phobias. This one woman couldn't *stand* buttons. Turns out, it's not the buttons at all, it's the fear of very small things teeming up, building up. It's the fear of a swarm. Of being taken over. Makes sense she swiped all of them, when you think of it like that.

HANNAH. Grandma did not swipe these buttons.

NESSA. Saturdays, at Balich's Five and Ten.

HANNAH. I remember that part, I do not remember stealing –

NESSA. She was all white gloves and lipstick.

HANNAH. High heels and stockings.

NESSA. She was all "just you try to give me crap" and she'd smile and chat with the other wives and when Balich wasn't looking? she'd sneak a button into her pocket.

HANNAH. Nessa.

NESSA. She did. I saw. Four years old. It was just me and her. White gloves and lipstick and her pinky finger easing one of those buttons into the cuff of her coat. In the car on the way home her face was on fire. "Mr. Balich had some ideas about me", she said. The first time she walked in Mr. Balich's, she said, Mr. Balich didn't know who he was dealing with. Mr. Balich thought she was a housekeeper, doing someone else's errands. One by one she played a riddle on him. She knew he didn't really see her that first time. She was invisible. One by one, she proved she wasn't that at all. She wasn't going to let this town overtake her. I'm sorry.

HANNAH. …me too. I don't know what to do, Nessa. The house, Miles, even opening the front door and stepping out of it, I don't –. I'm not good at any of this.

NESSA. Bullshit.

HANNAH. I'm so tired, Nessa, I have this coat of, coat of armor kind of and it's, it's…I don't know how she did any of it. Each button I find I want to hand right back. How she moved through the world when so much of it was saying you do not belong here, I don't know where she got the strength.

MILES. *(off)* MOM. MOM.

NESSA. GIVER A MINUTE, MILES.

NESSA. She never would've let you come back if she thought you'd get crushed by this place – Maybe we need to, let our guard down, enough. So it isn't so difficult. Like what if we don't brace for the swarm, what if we make it easier than that?

MILES. *(off)* MOM. MOOOOOOMMMM.

NESSA. MILES, GIVE IT A REST FOR GOD'S SAKE.

(*She touches* HANNAH's *cheek as she did in the swatting game before.*)

NESSA. You and me, Han.

MILES. MOM?

NESSA. *(calls)* I'm coming, Miles.

MILES. IT IS. IT IS: IT'S THE ICE CREAM TRUCK I NEED MONEY MOM I NEED –

(From almost nowhere we see an elderly woman.)

*(It is **MRS. DONOVAN**, much older.)*

MRS. DONOVAN. They're never really too old to take across your knee, are they?

*(**HANNAH** jumps.)*

HANNAH. Mrs. Donovan?

MRS. DONOVAN. Did I give you a start?

HANNAH. Well you usually announce yourself with a note.

MRS. DONOVAN. So sorry we couldn't make the picnic.

HANNAH. You shouldn't be here.

MRS. DONOVAN. It was sweet of you to invite us.

HANNAH. I thought, at the time, my grandmother would have wanted that/but –

MRS. DONOVAN. That's sweet, too, but it isn't true.

HANNAH. She liked you.

MRS. DONOVAN. She liked my husband, they were similar.

HANNAH. I'm going to call Mr. Donovan –

MRS. DONOVAN. With me she sent fruit cake. Every year, by Three Kings Day, there was always a fruit cake. We couldn't give fruitcake. How was I to afford fruitcake? She knew that.

*(**MRS. DONOVAN** notices the jar of buttons.)*

MRS. DONOVAN. Buttons?

*(**HANNAH** notices **MRS. DONOVAN**.)*

HANNAH. They were my grandmother's. She...collected them.

MRS. DONOVAN. A hobby.

HANNAH. Yes –

MRS. DONOVAN. How nice to have the time.

(*Turns to* HANNAH.)

We've got the communion coming up so we'll be needing you to move out by the first –

HANNAH. This is not your house.

MRS. DONOVAN. It's borrowed luck, that's what it is –

HANNAH. You can't just come in here demanding things. No matter what arrangements our grandparents made fifty years ago, this is house is ours now.

MRS. DONOVAN. Not to mention how this place skyrocketed. You do the math and it makes your head swell. My girls shared a bed.

HANNAH. Your "girls" are senior citizens now, they can buy their own beds.

MRS. DONOVAN. Cheeky.

HANNAH. Where's *Mr.* Donovan–?

MRS. DONOVAN. Useless. That's what Mr. Donovan amounts to.

(*She softens, sad.*)

My girls shared a bed and my boys had holes. At the elbows of their sweaters, in the soles of their shoes.

HANNAH. Mrs. Donovan?

MRS. DONOVAN. Borrowed. *Borrowed* there's an order to things. There's an order to who should get what and when and how and I, I…

(**MRS. DONOVAN** *looks to* **HANNAH**, *disoriented.*)

MRS. DONOVAN. Your head swells, it, it…

HANNAH. Mrs. Donovan?

(*The breeze.*)

(**MR. DONOVAN** *appears.*)

MR. DONOVAN. Patty, now, come now – (*to* HANNAH) I'm so sorry –

MRS. DONOVAN. (*to* HANNAH) There's a way things are supposed to work.

MR. DONOVAN. Please, Patty, let's not disturb –

MRS. DONOVAN. "A man wants to buy his own house, his own castle" that's what you said –

MR. DONOVAN. Patty, let's not discuss this here –

MRS. DONOVAN. *(As she busies with her things and produces a worn piece of paper).* Minute I read your grandfather had passed I knew it was time to set things right. Second I heard your voice on the line, inviting us to that memorial, I knew it was only a matter of time before it all came out, before the wills and the lawyers, what with your grandmother going so quick after, I knew it was time to get to the bottom of this. Straighten all this out. Our name is on this title, Joe.

HANNAH. *(taking the title)* Oh, oh no.

MRS. DONOVAN. This house is supposed to be coming to us.

REX. Milk and honey, you're right, there –

HANNAH. Is this real, Mr. Donovan?

JOE. Streets paved with pure gold my Dad used to say –

MRS. DONOVAN. Tell her what the good Doctor Taylor said to you about this title.

REX. – but six mouths –

MR. DONOVAN. Now that was fifty years ago now.

JOE. – Rooting around –

MRS. DONOVAN. Tell her what he said, Joe.

(**REX**'s *laughter rises, and he sits at the picnic table, drink in one hand. It is not entirely happy laughter. Also at the table is a young* **JOE DONOVAN**, *drink also in hand.*)

(It is fifty years earlier.)

(It is clear both men have had a few.)

REX. – I have one fellow, one fellow pays me in crab apples…and I wonder, what kind of country –

JOE. What was the war –

REX. – cause I thought I lifted us into better but I keep taking the long way home. You know why? Nights like Conference Night that's why.

JOE. Those nights, me and Patty, we're helter skelter running from room to room –

REX. At home I was King of Conference night. But Tasha's teacher here, Mrs. Brady, intimated, our girl can barely read. That Mrs. Brady made our girl out to be some ragamuffin just emerged from the soot and grime – At home conference night felt warm, Joe. Can I call you –?

JOE. Sure, sure –

(Wind billows.)

MRS. DONOVAN. What did you do?

REX. I don't want them growing thick skins.

JOE. Your girls will be alright. It's a special thing to have a way with words, like you and Mrs. Taylor.

MRS. DONOVAN. *What did you do?*

JOE. My youngest, Colleen, she's got a way. But Patty Ann's already got her folding up that washing. Already showed her how to tie the twine just so. Tight knot. Four years old.

REX. Six kids

JOE. there's a special place in heaven.

(REX raises a glass to JOE.)

It isn't easy for Patty Ann. We're not similar and, and I don't know how to to fix. Any of it. But I need you to know what you and me're doing, this is the one most true thing I've ever ever done. Even though my blood goes cold when I think about it all the kids, Patty Ann, everything –

MR. DONOVAN. I took what he gave, the extra he gave for the kids and I told Patty Ann the deal was still alive and kicking.

REX. *We're* similar, Joe. Wearing these thick skins and underneath we're dying. There's salt and brine clogging –.

(**REX** *takes out his bill fold.*)

HANNAH. What does that mean?

REX. From one sappy kid to another.

JOE. No, no, I couldn't.

REX. For those six, then.

(**REX** *gives* **JOE** *money, takes the new house title in one elegant gesture.*)

MRS. DONOVAN. Yes, what does that *mean?*

JOE. Oh, no, I couldn't. Take anything.

REX. Your name on the line as much as ours. Now that that title's transferred. I'm gonna place this right in Lucy's hand and I know her. She's gonna put it someplace so safe, probably hide it where not even I can find it sewn into a mattress, under a floorboard, pasted into a kitchen drawer, she, she

MR. DONOVAN. I took that extra and I used a little for Patty Ann, told her me and Rex Taylor had a deal, assured her I was making sure we got what we deserved.

REX. Milk and honey my ass you take that. No more twine.

MR. DONOVAN. But… sometimes on a summer night, I'd find myself up the hill, in this backyard, and your grandfather, your grandfather, he knew, he knew how hard it can be, and he'd say, take this, Joe, it's Sean's birthday next week. Take this, Joe, I hear Colleen made the honor roll –

MRS. DONOVAN. What are you saying?

MR. DONOVAN. Once I took some of it and took a class. Paid for the whole semester upfront with what he gave me. Sat and raised my hand, even asked, asked a question –. But I didn't finish, I couldn't –

MRS. DONOVAN. This house is ours –

HANNAH. No.

MRS. DONOVAN. Joe, I've got the title, Joe –

MR. DONOVAN. She got back from meeting Mrs. Taylor and well, I couldn't keep hiding from them John, your grandfather. It wasn't right –

MRS. DONOVAN. You agreed, you said after they died we would...

HANNAH. What happened, Mr. Donovan?

MR. DONOVAN. I signed it.

(MRS. DONOVAN *gasps.*)

MR. DONOVAN. I signed that title over to the Taylor's that night. Me and Rex went to John, and I transferred everything just like we promised. John even notarized it himself. After, to celebrate, we went up the hill, to this yard, where he gave me extra I never even asked for.

(HANNAH *nods, relief.*)

HANNAH. It was transferred.

MR. DONOVAN. Yes.

MRS. DONOVAN. No. No.

MR. DONOVAN. Jesus, the taxes alone on this place.

MRS. DONOVAN. I have it right here, I have proof. I tried to warn your grandmother – show her I had evidence –

MR. DONOVAN. And you add the electric and the oil; it would have buried us, this house.

MRS. DONOVAN. I deserve this house, not the Vitellos, not the Taylors.

MR. DONOVAN. *(to* HANNAH*)* I took the title that was no good anymore and I slipped it back into Patty Ann's top drawer.

MRS. DONOVAN. Jesus.

MR. DONOVAN. Between the stockings and a bar of Ivory soap. To keep the clothes smelling.

(MRS. DONOVAN *wags her head.*)

MR. DONOVAN. We saw in the paper they'd had passed, and then you called and Patty,

MRS. DONOVAN. Always by Three Kings, there it was.

MR. DONOVAN. Fifty years, how could I, how could I tell her I –

MRS. DONOVAN. Lied. You lied.

MR. DONOVAN. …I did. I'm so. I'm so sorry, I –. But the title your grandmother has, the date's good, it's after the one there.

HANNAH. But it's that we can't find our title anywhere.

(He indicates the paper in MRS. DONOVAN*'s hand.)*

MRS. DONOVAN. Three Kings.

MR. DONOVAN. Patty Ann –

MRS. DONOVAN. You owe me the very breath in your throat doing this to me, Joe.

MR. DONOVAN. Not enough punching in and punching out in the whole entire world could make this house ours.

*(*MRS. DONOVAN *wags her head.)*

MRS. DONOVAN. *(to herself)* You grow up and you think, you believe with every ounce of you that you're going to be better. You watch your mother rinse her stockings at night and you think that won't be me when I'm grown, I'll have more. You watch the neighbors use a pound of hamburg to feed six kids and you think that won't be my kids when I'm grown, I'll have more, I'll have so much more, but. Something. Something happens and you. It *is* you. It is you darning stockings and avoiding catching the butcher's eye at Mass because now it's you with the six kids and the open mouths and I don't understand what happened to the order.

MR. DONOVAN. Let's go home, Mrs. Donovan.

*(*MRS. DONOVAN *knocks over the jar suddenly, sending buttons onto the table, the ground.)*

MRS. DONOVAN. *(as she knocks the jar over)* She knew it was borrowed. She knew it. It was supposed to be us next, Joe. Not her.

(HANNAH goes to the jar, the buttons.)

MR. DONOVAN. Please excuse my wife –

(HANNAH tries to replace the fallen buttons to the jar.)

MRS. DONOVAN. After those English then the Irish *then* the Italians, then the blacks.

HANNAH. Go.

MRS. DONOVAN. My girls didn't share a bed just sos we'd get skipped over.

HANNAH. Go. Now.

MR. DONOVAN. Please excuse –

MRS. DONOVAN. I got skipped over, Joe. I got skipped over. I. I. I missed out, Joe. I. And now it's too late.

(MR. DONOVAN goes to her, soothes her, guides her away. Beat. MR. DONOVAN leads MRS. DONOVAN off, then turns to HANNAH.)

MR. DONOVAN. She was a lovely woman, your grandmother. I always thought, in another place, maybe, we would have gotten to…

MR. DONOVAN. Something there is that doesn't love a wall. Because I like to think. Winds of change –

(A car horn sounds again, then again.)

HANNAH. Go to your wife, Mr. Donovan.

(MR. DONOVAN looks at HANNAH.)

MR. DONOVAN. You'll find that title.

(A car horn.)

MR. DONOVAN. I should have made it easy for her.

HANNAH. Good bye, Mr. Donovan.

MR. DONOVAN. Goodbye.

(MR. DONOVAN goes. Beat. HANNAH surveys the table, the buttons, goes to gather them back into the jar.)

*(**RICH** enters, briefcase and jacket in hand. He and **HANNAH** look at each other.)*

*(**RICH** sits at the picnic table, opens his briefcase.)*

HANNAH. You just missed the circus, Rich, those Donovans –

(He pulls out all the mail from before.)

HANNAH. I – It's just so *much*, but I, I was gonna –

*(**MILES** enters, like a tornado.)*

MILES. Mom, Mom, Simon Greeley was just at the park and he says his mom says to tell you she sent his invitations last week and that I should have mine now do I have mine now? Maybe it's here and we don't know? Check again mom, check again. Pleeaase…

*(**RICH** and **HANNAH** look at each other.)*

MILES. And money for Italy Ice? Auntie Nessa had no money.

*(**HANNAH** goes to the pile, sorts through it, considers the envelopes, pulls out an invitation.)*

HANNAH. It. Must have gotten lost under. All that other mail.

MILES. *Yeah.*

HANNAH. We'll buy him a present this weekend.

*(**HANNAH** hands **MILES** the envelope.)*

*(**HANNAH** looks at **RICH** as **MILES** runs off.)*

MILES. Simon, *SIMON*, it's *here*. I got it.

*(**MILES** returns, goes to **RICH**.)*

*(**RICH** fishes into his pocket, gives ice cream money to **MILES**.)*

MILES. That's what Ise talking 'bout the Benjamins. SIMON, SIMON, I GOTS COLD HARD DIRTY CASH, SIMON.

*(**MILES** runs off.)*

RICH. He goes back Monday.

> *(HANNAH looks at RICH, nods.)*

Show those teachers what's what.

HANNAH. I don't know, Rich –

RICH. Act like we *belong* up in here.

HANNAH. We still don't have that title.

RICH. It's just a piece of paper Hannah. We'll find it.

HANNAH. I don't know if I can –

RICH. We live here. Yes?

> *(RICH kisses HANNAH. For real this time.)*

> *(RICH exits to the house.)*

> *(The breeze.)*

> *(LUCY appears.)*

> *(HANNAH and LUCY look at one another.)*

> *(Quiet.)*

> *(HANNAH picks up the jar of buttons, holds it out to LUCY.)*

LUCY. You earned it Keep it.

HANNAH. Yes.

> *(LUCY nods.)*

LUCY. Yes.

> *(HANNAH looks down at the jar, then up to LUCY again, but LUCY has gone. HANNAH looks down at the jar as wind blows, warm, clean, rolling.)*

End of Play